A Nickel
In My Shoe

My story of abuse, survival,
faith and forgiveness

By: S.B. Jenkins

ISBN: 0615495613
ISBN-13: 9780615495613

DEDICATION

In loving memory of my sister Karen whom I miss and love so very much

Little Sister

My little sister, my very best friend
I will love you till the end

Holding your hand, watching you die
Can not protect you this time, all I can do is cry

When we were small, I didn't mind taking the fall
This fall I can not change, this fall I can not take away

This beating I can not take for you, Lord knows I've begged
He knows I've pleaded, Oh God this can't be true

Just a little time is left, that's all that is needed
To tell you how much I love you, and it should be me dying,
Not you

Who will I laugh with, and talk to? Who will guide me through?
Who will I share my deepest secrets with?
There's no one like you

Little sister, my very best friend
I will love you till the end
Holding your hand, watching you die, you must be so afraid
I feel so helpless, all I can do is cry

Can not protect you from your pain
This is the one that I can not take away
I will miss you and love you, till my own dying day

To have you back, anything I would give
In my heart, you will forever live

Love you with all of my heart, Susan

CONTENTS

PROLOGUE

On a cold dark April morning, a baby girl was born. She was all of four pounds, and was so thin you could see clear through her skin. She was lucky to be alive because babies born prematurely in the early 1960's usually didn't survive. They lacked surfactant- a protein that the lungs need to be able to expand in order to breathe.

I wonder...when this little newborn baby's mother held her for the first time, and while gazing into her child's eyes, did she say, "Someday I'm going to beat you until you are black and blue," or did she say, "I'm going to pour caustic liquid in your ear someday, so you'll be deaf," or did she say, "I'm going to viciously whip you all over your second- degree sunburned body, and leave you to rot without food, water, or pain medicine for days," or did she say...

I also wonder what this baby's father said when he *finally* made it to the hospital from the bar room to see his new baby daughter. Did he pick her up and while looking into her innocent newborn eyes say, "I'm not going to feed you, because I don't care if you starve," or did he say, "someday, when you need emergency medical treatment, I'm going to give you a terrible beating for getting sick and inconveniencing me, throw you on the couch and leave you there alone- without food, water, or medicine for days on end," or did he say...

That little baby girl was me. Born too early and always sick, my mother made sure to criticize me about that every chance she got for all of my life. She would also complain about how much I cried when I was an infant, and how I *never* slept.

When my mother brought my newborn sister Karen home from the hospital, she placed her in her crib. That baby was annoying! She wouldn't stop crying. I got up from my chair, walked into her room, crawled into the crib and *slapped* her in the face as hard as I could. Her face turned beet red. I didn't understand why she didn't 'shut up'- she only cried harder! All I knew was that whenever *I* cried, my mother would slap *me* in the face to make me stop, so, I wanted to stop this new baby from crying and that was the *only* way I knew how. Crying wasn't allowed. Period. I was only two and a half years old.

For as far back as I can remember, my mother would tease and taunt me. She would play on my weaknesses. She would tell me that my grandmother, "Nana", wasn't coming over to visit us anymore because I was a bad girl, and Nana didn't love me anymore. All the while Nana would be hiding behind a door. My mother would laugh hysterically as I cried and sobbed because she knew how much I loved my grandmother, which was more then life itself.

When the maxi coats came in style, I wanted one so very badly. I would put on my mothers coat because it came down to my ankles, and pretend it was a maxi coat. I would then prance up and down the street. I thought I looked pretty stylish, but in reality I looked ridiculous! The coat was actually so long that I tripped and tore my knee up pretty badly. My father gave me a beating that day for injuring my knee. That was another thing- getting hurt was also against the rules.

The next day, after arriving home from school, my mother announced that she bought my sister's Karen and Mary a maxi coat, but not me. She said I was a bad girl and didn't deserve one, and that my sisters were good girls, and they did. I had to watch both of my sister's prance around in their new coats. My mother sat there and laughed at me while I was forced to choke back my tears.

After we went to bed at night, my mother would come in and threaten us- she would say, "If you girls don't get right to sleep, the 'beesh' (boogie man) is going to come out from under the bed and eat you!" We would lay there terrified to death-in turn, making it practically impossible to fall asleep *(To this day I can't hang my feet out of the bed, I need to be completely covered with blankets.)*

What my mother found humorous, at my expense, I found heart wrenching, and at times- terrifying. She made me feel utterly worthless, and pathetic. She always told me that I should be ashamed of myself. And I was. She even told me that God didn't like me. Every time it thundered, she said that God was mad at me because I was a bad girl.

There was nothing that I could do well enough- there wasn't anything that I could do right. No matter what I did I couldn't please her. No matter how hard I tried I couldn't make my mother love me.

INTRODUCTION

My story is one of severe abuse, neglect and bullying, as well as faith, survival and forgiveness. It is one of profound sorrow, love and hate, and most of all, of courage and hope.

I grew up in a time where whites hated blacks, and blacks hated whites, or at least they were *supposed* to hate each other. I didn't. That's why it was so difficult for me to understand why I was picked on and beat up after school almost everyday by an African American girl that absolutely hated me for no reason at all- except for the color of my skin. I didn't understand it then, and I don't understand it now. I have friends of all races, colors, and creeds. I respect and learn from each and every one of them. I see beyond color. You might say I'm "blind" in that respect. One might think after being bullied at school that arriving home would have been a relief- after all, everyone needs their safe haven. There was no safe place for me to run to. Home was just as terrifying of an environment as school was.

My father was an extreme alcoholic and severely abusive to my mother-physically as well as mentally. Although my father beat me and my sisters for insignificant reasons such as getting a skinned knee, or putting our feet on the car's seat or couch, he didn't beat us often- but, he wasn't home all that much either. He was out most every night searching for something that he thought other woman and alcohol would bring him…peace within his soul. I don't think he ever found it.

When I was very young, I adored my father. He was funny, and fun loving- A "good time charlie" so to speak. And why shouldn't he have been? He had no worries- he had no responsibilities. That was my mother's job.

He would dance and sing to me..."Brown Eyed Girl," "Wake Up Little Suzie," and "Run Around Sue," while he snapped his fingers, and tapped his feet, or played air guitar. He made me feel special. My father would tell funny jokes that were actually meant for adults-*he* would laugh, while my sister's and I would be bewildered. But he also had a dark side-he had a temper and would just *snap* for no reason at all.

My feelings for him were a combination of fear coupled with love. (Freud would have had a field day with that statement!) I didn't realize that he was an unfit parent and could care less if we had the basic necessities of life. My mother made sure we had what we needed as far as food, shelter and clothing, at least when we were very young.

Over the years I grew to see the kind of man my father truly was. I removed my "rose colored glasses" one might say. But instead of hating or resenting him, I felt *sorry* for him. He was an empty man with a lost soul. My father died never finding what he was searching for all of his life...whatever it was, I hope he found it in heaven.

I don't think my mother *meant* to be abusive, I surmise that she had some psychiatric issues that were never dealt with, coupled with the fact that she didn't know any better due to the lack of a proper role model and education. She had displaced anger that she didn't know how to deal with, along with an insurmountable amount of stress. She must have felt as if the weight of the world was on her shoulders, as well as helpless, because she felt that there wasn't anything she could do about it.

I felt differently toward my mother than I did my father. I feared her as well, but what was different is that I didn't feel much love for her. She tricked me too often. Just when I thought she accepted me and loved me, she would do something to counteract it. It was almost as if she would say to herself, *"Oh yeah, don't let my wall down, I don't like her."* Why, you ask? Because she resented the idea that I loved my father- that's why.

My poor sister Mary didn't make it out alive- but *I* was determined to survive- I was determined to succeed, even if it *was* against all odds.

From the very young age of five, I dreamed of becoming a nurse one day. Many obstacles stood in my way- my lack of education and my tremendous fear of math. The people that were supposed to love and encourage me the most were trying to break me by telling me things such as I was too worthless and stupid to *ever* succeed in college, or in life for that matter. The more those nasty people laughed at me and told me I couldn't make it through, the more determined I became to succeed, and I did. I became a registered nurse. It was the most difficult thing that I ever accomplished in my life, for the reasons listed above, as well as at that particular time in my life I was going through a very difficult divorce, left homeless with four children to feed without a dime in my pocket, as well as trying to care for a terminally ill parent-my mother.

My mother certainly mellowed more as she grew older. We eventually became best friends. I know it seems that I am making excuses for her behavior, but I'm not. There *is* no good enough excuse for abuse of any kind. What I can tell you is that I have forgiven her for all she has done to me, and believe it or not, I would give *anything* to have her back. The love and affection that she couldn't give to me when I was a child, she made up for later in life.

My story of severe maltreatment (unfortunately) isn't new- but like everyone's, it is unique. Abuse and neglect happens in homes all around the world every second of every day to children from all walks of life, from newborn infants to teenagers and beyond. But when *you* are the one it's happening to... you feel so lost and helpless, and the world feels like an unkind and lonesome place. You believe that there is no end in sight, and the fear you feel rolling around in the pit of your stomach is almost as unbearable as the pain, humiliation and suffering that is being inflicted upon your body, mind and soul. You survive on hope...that someone will notice... that someone will care...that someone will have the courage to save you. In your thoughts you scream, hoping someone will hear your cries; begging to be rescued-I know, because I felt that exact way every second of every day for all of my young life.

Abuse comes in many forms- physical, emotional, sexual, and neglect.

"Historically, children were considered chattel. Parents could raise and punish their children whatever way they wanted to, without reprisal from authorities.

Many states had no laws governing child abuse. In only the severest cases were children protected- under Animal Cruelty Laws. Up until 1974, child abuse and neglect was hardly recognized. This is when Congress began to allocate monies for the removal of children from their abusive homes. This was reserved for the most severe abuse and neglect cases." (The University of Arizona Child Advocacy Clinic)

"The statistics on abuse are alarming. In 1960, 64,000 cases of suspected child abuse were reported in the United States. In

1970, there were 72,000 cases, in 1980 1,100,000, in 1990, 2,400,000, and 3,000.000 cases reported in 1993." (1998 The American Academy of Experts in Traumatic Stress, Inc.)

"In 2007, a report of child abuse was made every ten seconds. Four children die every day as a result of child abuse—three are under the age of four. Over 30% of women in prison, as well as over 60% of people in drug rehabilitation report being abused as children. The estimated annual cost of child abuse and neglect in the United States is over $104 billion a year." (Child Help Inc.)

Much thanks to increased education and awareness, the incidence of child abuse reports have slightly decreased- however, not enough. The *only* way to combat ignorance is through education. We must increase awareness, not only here in the United States, but around the world, in order to eradicate child abuse and neglect.

CHAPTER ONE

RUNNING FOR MY LIFE

Terri Lyn is chasing me again. She won't let up! This time she has at least ten people trailing behind her. They are big, black, mean, and scary looking. They are all shouting at me. My head is so dizzy and numb with fear that I can't understand a word they are saying. I'm running out of breath, but what's worse is that I'm running out of time. I think this is the day I am going to die, or at least, *wish* I would…right about now would be good. Maybe she will kill me today. Then it will all be over-all the fear, hurt, and pain in my life. Nobody would miss me anyway.

Gees, usually she's alone when she beats me up everyday. But today is different. Today I wouldn't give her my lunch, *(she took it anyway and told me she was going to hurt me bad)*. She is mad! I don't just mean angry, I mean 'mad' in every sense of the word. The trouble started in first grade, in Inter-City Elementary School, where I first met Terri Lyn. Black with a big Afro, she was short in stature, and somewhat on the chunky side. She acted mean and tough, and said a lot of bad words. She didn't like white people, especially me.

1

A NICKEL IN MY SHOE

I didn't know why there were bad feelings between people of different colors. I couldn't understand where the tension and hatred came from. How could I understand- I was only five-years-old. I wasn't raised to judge people based on the color of their skin. I even had a little boyfriend. His name was Shawn. Half black and half white, he was as cute as could be with olive colored skin, light hair and freckles.

Shawn was the only light in my life...everything else was dark-dark and painful. Terri Lyn didn't like the fact that I liked a boy of mixed race- and he liked me.

"Gimmee your lunch *bitch*!" Terri Lyn screeched after the lunch monitor left to sneak a smoke outside. I could feel my face turning red with embarrassment and my head tingle with fear. The lunchroom would go silent when she bullied me, which was everyday-Monday thru Friday, before, during and after school. Most days she'd wait for me by my bus after school. I would hide from her, miss my bus, then have to walk home, or should I say get my butt kicked all the way home.

I couldn't get away from Terri Lyn. It seemed as if it was her mission in life to torment me. I wished just for once that I could eat my lunch. I was *so* hungry everyday. One might think that the other kids would start to bully me as well, but they didn't. I guessed that they all must have felt sorry for me on one hand. And on the other, they were thanking God it was *me* she was terrorizing, and not *them*.

Terri Lyn went to great lengths to stay on my tail. For example, in the beginning of third grade I was tested and placed in the most intelligent math class. So was she. In order to get away from her I did poorly on purpose in order to move down to the intermediate level. So did she. I did the same again, performed poorly to get to the final level, known as the dummy math class. So did she. I just couldn't get away from her no matter how hard I tried. Whenever Terri Lyn was near I became sick to my stomach. I would become nauseated, and felt as if I could vomit. I didn't understand why.

I'm runnin'...every few seconds I would turn my head to look at the mob behind me. Terri Lyn is leading the pack. They are gaining on me, and it seems for every one step I run, my house gets fifty steps farther away. Oh my God, I have to get them off of my tail. They can't follow me home. If my mother ever caught wind of this she would take Terri Lyn's side and blame all of this on me. My mother would proceed to embarrass me further by beating me in front of Terri Lyn and her gang, just like she threatened to do to me after my teacher called her on the phone and complained to her that I asked to go to the bathroom much too often. My mother warned me that if I ever asked to go to the bathroom again she would come to my school, pull my pants down in front of the whole class, put me over her knee and "spank my ass." And I believed her. She liked to do that sort of thing to my sister's and I, especially when people were there to watch. She thrived on having an audience when she hit us. She thought humiliating us was humorous. I could sense that it made her feel powerful, and in control.

Suddenly, I feel a hand grab a hold of my long brown hair. Terri Lyn swung me around. "Wait a minute, wait a minute Terri Lyn, I...I...I... have money. I have a nickel in my shoe. I'll give it to you if you all just don't hurt me," I blurted.

"O.k. little bitch, get it!" she yelled.

I have never been as terrified in my life as I was at that moment because there *was* no nickel in my shoe. I didn't know what to do next. I proceeded to bend down as if to get the nickel out of my shoe. All of a sudden, someone or something picked up my arm, my fingers began to curl into a fist, my arm went back, and I punched Terri Lyn square in the eye with all of my might. I watched as she fell to the ground. I stood there frozen for a few seconds just looking at my fist, not knowing who or what possessed me to punch her. I turned to look at Terri Lyn for a split second. She was lying sprawled out on the ground. The gang gathered around her. I think I knocked her out! Oh boy, now I was *really* in trouble. I ran home as fast as my little feet could carry me.

That night, after I went to bed, I prayed…I prayed for the Good Lord to take me in my sleep. I *did* wake up the next day. I vomited.

CHAPTER TWO

SOMETHING'S WRONG
WITH MARY

I was scrawny and undersized for my age. I had long dark brown straggly, curly hair, light brown eyes and fair skin with freckles, which kids in school poked fun at me for. Everyday they would ask me if I was sick because my high cheekbones made my face look gaunt, and my dark hair made my skin appear to be very pale.

I was, however, extremely bright. In fact, I was the only kid in my class that could read effortlessly. My first grade teacher would ask me to read the book *"Tip and Mitten"* to the class most every day while she went on break. I also helped the other kids in my class learn their alphabet, and with their reading assignments.

My handwriting was also exceptional. I won two awards in first and second grade. I also won every Spelling Bee except for one. In third grade, the entire class was asked to decipher notes while a teacher played them on her violin. I had no clue what this was all about, but I made my note choices, and handed them in to the teacher. One day my mother received a notice that I was one of three students out of the entire third grade class of 120 that passed the test. I was then offered free violin lessons. When my mother rented a violin for me, I was thrilled! I learned to play the instrument very quickly, and enjoyed it immensely. Unfortunately, my mother could no longer afford the dollar a week for the violin rental, and I had to quit my lessons.

I had two sister's - Mary and Karen. There was about three year's age difference between us. I was the middle child. Maybe that explains why I was quite often pushed aside.

Mary was the oldest. She was exceptionally intelligent, but she was odd to say the least. There was definitely something wrong with her personality, I just didn't know what it was at the time. I didn't know it had a name.

There were times when I overheard my mother talking on the phone to her friends about Mary. She would brag about how Mary stood up in her crib at three months, was crawling at four months, and talking fluently when she was only one and a half. But my mother neglected to mention that Mary *never* liked to be touched or cuddled, or that when my mother tried to pick her up and hold her on her lap, she would scream and fight to get down. My mother never told anyone how Mary *never* smiled. There were other very strange things about my sister, among them was that she didn't feel physical pain. The only emotion she would show was anger, and the only feeling she felt was hate.

Mary was wicked, in the evil sense of the word. She would terrorize Karen and me, especially me. She *hated* me. She once dangled Karen upside down by her ankles out of the window of our second floor apartment all because I said that I didn't want to play school with her. The more Karen screamed with fright, the more Mary would laugh, shake her and pretend that she was going to drop her by letting her hands start to slip from around Karen's ankles. I was so small all I could do was watch and scream, cry and beg. Mary would tell me if I tried to help Karen that she would drop her and then she would be dead. She certainly knew how to manipulate me. Mary was very aware of how much I loved my baby sister and she took advantage of it. She realized early on that Karen was my weak spot.

I was screaming, "Please Mary, I'll do anything you want… *anything*, just tell me what it is you want, but please don't drop Karen…please…!"

Mary responded with, "I want you to play school with me." I agreed, and only then did she drag Karen back through the window. I had mixed emotions at that particular moment-relief that Karen was alive and great fear, because I played school with Mary before. This was another one of her sadistic torture games…but that was o.k. I kept my word. Karen was safe, and that was all that mattered to me.

At the other end of our apartment sat what we called the 'empty room.' It was a room that my mother couldn't afford to heat so that is where our toys were stored. Mary made me sit for what seemed like hours, in front of the chalkboard in the empty room. I was so cold and had to pee so badly, but I didn't dare ask. I was the student and she was the teacher. She would give me a word to spell, and I best get it right or I'd pay the price…slapped with the ruler she held, and kicked. I remember her telling me to spell the word "hospital." I know that I spelled it correctly, H-O-S-P-I-T-A-L. She would say that I didn't spell it right. This was her excuse for torturing me, which also included belittling me.

A NICKEL IN MY SHOE

"You're dumb and stupid," she would yell in my face. Then BAM, down came the ruler, and up came her foot.

Mary was very careful to hit and kick me only on my clothing so that my mother couldn't see the bruises and red marks. This was kind of silly because no one would be able to tell who made what mark and where. I got hit by from both of them almost everyday. Being three years younger than Mary, I was no match for her-mentally or physically. I had to sit on that chair and take whatever she had to dish out, without moving an inch or uttering a sound. She told me if I moved or cried the slaps and kicks would get harder, and that she would throw Karen out the window. She then proceeded to tell me that if I told anyone about our game, she would throw *me* out of the window along with Karen.

Mary felt that she was different than Karen and I because she didn't look like us. She felt as if she didn't belong. Mary had my father's olive colored skin and long black wavy hair. She had a set of ebony eyes that would stop people dead in their tracks. Her eyes were as black as night, you couldn't even see the pupil in them. They were dead and cold, similar to sharks eyes. There was nothing in them, just endless emptiness. Karen and I both had my mother's fair Irish skin tone with light brown hair and eyes to match. Mary resented this.

Mary was full of hatred. She never smiled. She must have felt broken. She was immune to the daily beatings with the belt. Most of the beatings she received were because she was mean to Karen and I, which in turn made our punishments from Mary more and more sadistic as time went on. Quite often she got hit with the belt because she would tell my mother how much she hated her, and wished she (my mother) were dead. Mary had balls; she told it like it was without holding back. She didn't

care. She refused to give my mother the satisfaction of screaming and crying when she was getting hit. Over time, Mary just
became apathetic, with a flat affect and a violent temper.

The abuse had a different effect on me than it did on Mary. I
became afraid of everyone. I felt as is if I was going to be blamed
and punished for everything that ever went wrong. I felt as if
everything was *my* fault and that I couldn't do anything right.
I suffered from constant nausea caused by a feeling of fear that
lived in the pit of my stomach. I thought that this feeling was
normal because it never went away. I became depressed. I guess
you could say I became chronically sad, and suicidal (if *wishing*
for death constitutes a suicidal tendency, I don't know).

My Nana taught me that if I asked the Good Lord for *anything*, he would provide it. He disappointed me day after day,
year after year, because I only asked him for one thing everyday
and that was to take me to Heaven. I didn't know much about
Heaven, but I knew it had to be a better place than the one I
was in. I didn't understand why he wouldn't answer my prayer.
My mother was right, even God didn't want me. The feelings
of hopelessness and doom would haunt me for many years to
come.

CHAPTER THREE

MY LITTLE SISTER, MY ANGEL

My baby sister, Karen, was an angel. She had long brown shiny hair, with sparkling big brown eyes, and a smile that melted my heart. She had a very special air about her. She was calm and easy going. She appeared to be happy, or at least, not scared all of the time like I was. Karen hardly ever got in trouble, or hit by my mother. I would have to say she was my mothers' favorite child.

Karen was the only one of us who ever had a birthday party. Her Godparents would host it for her every year. I think I was more excited about all the birthday presents than Karen was. I would even try to help her open them, but my mother would elbow me out of the way. She did the same thing when it came time to take pictures... shove me out of the way as if I was a dog wanting to be pet at the most inconvenient time.

Karen and I grew to be very close. I loved her with all of my heart and soul. I always felt a strange need to protect her. When she got hit I could feel that big ball of fear in my stomach wake up and start rolling around. I could equate the feeling to a bunch of snakes crawling around in my stomach. I would gladly take the blame for anything and everything Karen did wrong so that she wouldn't get hit. I didn't mind being her whipping boy. My mother favored Karen though, and that was a good thing. It was Mary and me that got abused the worst, at least *most* of the time.

One night, I was lying beside my mother on the couch. We were watching her favorite television show called *Mission Impossible.* I couldn't understand what was going on in the show, but my mother sure liked it.

Karen was playing and singing on the floor beside us. She was only three-years-old. She was just a baby. My mother repeatedly told her to shut up. Karen didn't *shut up* after being told to do so. She continued to quietly sing and play. My mother summoned her over.

"I told you to shut up ten times. Now get your ass over here!"

Karen, very slowly, began to inch her way over to my mother. My mother got extremely angry. Through gritted teeth, she repeated, "I said get your ass over here NOW!"

Karen slowly continued to inch her way toward us. I was so scared. I began to beg my mother not to hurt her, but I was pleading to deaf ears. My mother reached out and grabbed Karen by the middle of her shirt, bunched it up between all of her fingers, and began to slap her in the face, repeatedly.

"I told you to shut up, didn't I? *slap.* When I tell you to shut up you better SHUT UP! *slap.* Stop that crying! *slap.* I'll give you something to cry about!" *slap.* Karen was crying so hard that her face was crying, her mouth was wide open, as wide as could be, but no sound was coming out.

I couldn't stand watching Karen get hit. My stomach felt so sick. I was crying for the pain and humiliation that my baby sister was suffering. My mother wouldn't stop slapping Karen in the face, even though I was begging and pleading with her to. I was frantic, and so desperate to make her stop. I had to think of something FAST…I knew what would make her stop, I blurted out, "I'm gonna tell Daddy on you when he gets home!

It worked. My mother let her go. She turned to me and I could see both fear and anger in her tiger yellow eyes. I knew what I just said to save Karen would be to my detriment, but that was o.k. as long as she wasn't hurting her anymore. I didn't care what she did to me at that point. I'll gladly take the slaps in the face for my little sister, that couldn't hurt any more than my heart already did.

My mother grabbed me and shook me. She told me that she would *kill* me if I told my father. Then, to my amazement, she let me go. I jumped off of the couch, and ran into the bedroom where Karen was hiding. I picked her up and held her close. Her face was so red.

"I'm so sorry Karen," I said. "I'm so sorry I couldn't stop her sooner."

My heart felt as if it was bleeding. I loved Karen so much. There are no words to express the love I felt for my baby sister. I actually felt her pain but the pain wasn't in my face, it was in my heart. I wanted so desperately to protect her. I promised her that when I was old enough, on my next (sixth) birthday, I would get a job as a nurse, and we would run away together, and live in a house of our own where no one would be able to hurt us ever again. *(Whenever I visited my Nana, I would sneak off with the job section in the local newspaper and call all the 'Nurse wanted' ads and ask if I could have a job. Needless to say, I couldn't keep my promise to my sister).*

My father finally came stumbling through the front door- late, and not from work, because he didn't work. He was drunk- as usual. I blurted out to him what my mother had done to Karen, knowing full well the consequence, but I didn't care. She had to pay for hurting my little sister. I saw his tongue come out of the side of his mouth and he would bite it, like he did when he was about to hit me (or anyone).

I knew she was going to get it now! He picked my mother up off the couch as if she was a rag doll, beating her from one end of the house to the other. Usually, when he hit her, it would make me feel scared and sorry for her-but not this time. Not tonight. I was glad. She got what she deserved after hurting and humiliating Karen the way she did. Nobody will harm my little sister and get away with it as long as I'm alive.

CHAPTER FOUR

DADDY'S HOME

My father's name was Jacob Robert, but everyone called him Bobby. People would tell him that he looked like Charles Bronson, he liked when people said that about him. He was an extremely vain man, with an ego the size of the moon.

My father was one of ten children; six boys and four girls. He was considered the black sheep, because he was the only one who led an empty and troubled life. His short temper would always get him into trouble, and his love for woman and alcohol would prevent him from having a normal family life.

My grandparents emigrated here from Italy when they were just newlyweds. They waited until they moved to America to start their family. They had high hopes of success here in the states, however, my grandfather died of a heart attack when my father was only eight- shattering any hopes for a prosperous future for the family. They all seemed to fair well in life despite the economic hardships they encountered, everyone except for my father that is.

He was an extremely handsome man with olive skin and dark brown slicked back hair. Woman loved him, and he loved them right back. (*I don't think he would know the true meaning of the word love even if it snuck up behind him and bit him in his rear-end).* My father was also a drunk and a womanizer, who cheated nightly with any whore at the bar that was willing to buy him drinks. He would go on drinking binges for days on end with any tramp that would have him. He couldn't hold a steady job because of his temper, and spent most of his days and nights at the bar.

While my father was out boozing it up and whore chasing, my mother was slaving away in a jewelry factory on the night shift for minimum wage so that she could provide the basic necessities of life for her children-all because my father wouldn't.

My mother tried hard to fit into a society where women didn't work outside of the home. It must have been very stressful for her. She had a difficult life. My mother was trying to feed three kids, pay the rent, and contend with a husband that would beat her for any reason or no reason at all. Heck, if he walked in and caught her on the telephone, he would fly into a jealous rage and start accusing her of talking to another man. And yes, you guessed it, she caught a beating.

My father was no coward. He didn't just pick on woman and children like most weenie abusers do. No, he was a *real* man. He didn't care who he fought with, or what their size was. He had a short fuse and a terrible temper.

One day we were sitting at a red light down on Eddie Street in Providence. The light turned green at which point my father began to proceed through the intersection. A man, about middle age, decided to run his red light while speeding out of the side street on the right of us, cutting my fathers' car off. I saw the tongue come out of my fathers' mouth, and thought

"Oh no, this man is in trouble, this poor man is going to get a beating."

My father caught up with him at the next red light. While they were both stopped there, my father got out of his car, went to the driver's side door of the man that cut us off. My father opened his door, dragged him out of his car and kicked the living daylights out of that poor man who lay unconscious and bloody on the ground. My sisters and I huddled together in the back seat. Karen and I were crying and Mary just stared off into space. My father got back into our car, and he drove off as if nothing ever happened.

There was one particular incident that I will *never* forget. It all happened one Christmas Eve in 1967. Oh how I wished for a Thumbelina doll. She was my favorite. I didn't care if Santa brought me anything else. That's all I wanted for Christmas. We were so excited. Even Mary seemed to be excited about Christmas. It was hard to tell. Mary didn't talk much, unless it was to call one of us a name, or to threaten one of us.

Christmas and birthdays were the only times of year that we received anything extra, in the way of toys. My mother and father went all out for us girls at Christmas time. I don't know how they managed to give us a Christmas *(I would hear my mother talking on the phone with her girlfriend Bernice, about how worried she was because she couldn't come up with the $12.00 for the rent that week)* but they, or should I say, *she*, somehow managed.

Christmas was a special time of year for my family. We would either take a trip to Edaville Railroad to visit Santa, or go to LaSalette Shrine to visit the tomb where Jesus was laid to rest. Sometimes we would visit both. Some years we attended midnight mass on Christmas Eve at the Cathedral in

A NICKEL IN MY SHOE

Providence. The Christmas of 1967, however, would be very different.

My mother had an extra special surprise this year... Santa Claus was coming to visit *US*. We must be special!! I thought. Mary, Karen and I were all in bed, tossing and turning. My mother allowed us sleep in her bed this particular night. Her bedroom was off the living room, where we could hear Santa come in. I heard noises on the roof. "What was that?" I think Rudolph and all the reindeer landed on the roof! Karen and Mary heard it too. Oh my God, I'm so excited I think I'm going to faint! I thought.

Next I hear, "HO, HO, HO, Merry Christmas." Santa was walking up our stairs! He walked through the front door. The three of us came running out to greet him.

"Santa...Santa...I love you so much!" I said.

"Have you been good girls this year?" Santa asked.

"Oh yes Santa yes!!! We've been good!" We all shrieked as we were jumping up and down. Santa had a huge sack of toys with him. I asked him if that was for all the girls and boys in the world.

"No," he said. "These presents are *all* for you girls."

The three of us continued to jump up and down in excitement. Even Mary!

"O.k.," Santa said, "Who is going to be the first one to sit on my lap?"

We all started screaming, "Me, Me, Me...! Right about then the front door bursts open.

"And who the fuck are you?" my father snarled. I felt the blood rush from my face. My mother yelled at us to "get in the bedroom quick....run!" We climbed into bed. I was scared to death. "Daddy *can't* hurt Santa...he will be mad at us and we won't get any presents," I said. We all got out of bed and opened the door just a crack. We heard my father asking my mother, "Is this your boyfriend? Is this the guy you're fucking? You whore!" He lunged at Santa. They knocked over the Christmas tree. I couldn't help myself; I darted out of the bedroom and jumped on my fathers' back. I was yelling at my father, "Leave Santa alone! Leave Santa alone!" My mother quickly tried to pry me off my fathers' back.

My father was so intent on hurting this man in the Santa suit that I don't think he realized that I was even on his back. My mother carried me back in to the bedroom where my sister's were. The police came and arrested my father, and Santa was taken to the hospital. When we woke up the next morning and walked out into the living room where the broken tree lay, we saw our toys. I did get the Thumbelina doll that I wanted so very badly. However, it didn't mean anything to me anymore. All I could think about was Santa and how sorry I felt for him, because I knew the pain and sadness he must have been feeling. *(Santa turned out to be my mother's girlfriend's boyfriend. She told me in later years, that he was an elderly man, and that my father hurt him very badly that night, both mentally as well as physically).*

My father was a sore loser. He had to win at everything, every game and every fight. My mother tried her best to avoid playing card games with him. The prize for winning a card game against my father was a terrible beating.

"Oh no, they're playing cards," Mary said. I could feel my stomach start to turn, and my heart felt as if it dropped to my feet-and someone tied a knot in my stomach.

My sister's and I shared a room; all three of us actually shared a bed. Our room was off of the kitchen so it was very easy to hear what was going on at the kitchen table. At first I heard laughter. I could tell my mother was nervous. She had to stroke his ego all through the game. She would say things like, "Oh Bobby, you're such a good card player, you should join a card club," or "Oh Bobby, you're winning so far. I know you are going to win this game." *So far, so good*, I thought. I started to feel at ease. Then it happened. My mother won the game. I know she didn't mean to. I know she was trying hard not to, but she did. When you are out of cards, you are out of cards.

"You cheated! you fuckin' bitch!" my father screamed. "No, I didn't mean to win, honest," she said in a weak, shaky voice. "Please Bobby, don't," she begged. *(She must have seen the tongue come out the side of his mouth).*

I heard the chair that my father was sitting in fly out from under him, across the kitchen and into the hutch cabinet. The knick-knacks crashed to the floor. He lunged at her. The sounds of punches, banging and screaming were so loud that I couldn't block them out, no matter how hard I held my ears. Finally it was over. That beating seemed as if it went on forever. All I hear now are the sounds of my father running out the front door, and my mother crying as she picked up the broken glass and furniture. This fight gave my father an excuse to leave, and go off drinking and whoring around for another few days. Not that he needed an excuse-but this is how he justified it, if he even cared enough to. My mother had such tremendous stress. She felt trapped- maybe that's the reason we were such a burden, maybe that's why she resented us.

I hated when my father left the house. I felt insecure and scared of my mother. As abusive as my father was to my mother, he wasn't *as* abusive to us girls, in a physical sense anyway. She hit us less when he was around. Aside from my Nana, my mother's mother, I loved my father with all of my heart, which happened to hurt whenever he went away. My mother resented this. I was certainly punished for it throughout my life. She couldn't understand why I loved a man who didn't care enough to provide the basic life necessities for his family-beat and cheated on my mother and was totally selfish. What my mother didn't understand was that I had no concept of any of that. All I knew at that young age is that he was my father and I loved him unconditionally.

CHAPTER FIVE

YOU LOOK JUST LIKE YOUR MOTHER

My mother, Paige, was stunningly beautiful. She had gorgeous tiger yellow eyes, fair skin and long dark brown hair. Petite and very shapely, most women were envious of her-especially one of my father's sisters- she was *extremely* jealous of her. I don't blame my aunt. I think she was born looking old and dumpy. She was ugly, on the inside as well as on the outside.

My aunt thought that none of her brothers could do *any* wrong. If one of the wives caught a beating, then they must have done something to deserve it.

Once, my uncle's wife kicked him out of the house after a fight. My aunt went over to their house, took off her high heel shoe, and proceeded to hit my uncles' wife in the head with it.

My Aunt Hilda was especially cruel. She would tell me in a high-pitched squeaky singing voice *"you look just like your mother."* I knew that couldn't be good because she didn't like my mother. Not because of how she treated us girls, but because of her beauty.

A NICKEL IN MY SHOE

One night my father's mother, *"Granny"* was babysitting for me. Two of my aunts were there visiting her. While playing outside I fell and skinned my knee on the pavement. It was bleeding. (*Thank God my father wasn't there- whenever we got injured he would beat us than put a band-aid on it later*). I was crying, "It's bloodin' it's bloodin' help! help!" The nicer one of my aunts picked me up and said, "Hush hush, it will be okay. I'll put some medicine on your boo boo, and it will be all better." I started to calm down. I felt as if everything would be all right. The aunt that disliked my mother the most said to me, "I have two kinds of medicine, iodine, and mercurochrome. So...do you want the medicine that stings, or do you want the medicine that doesn't sting?" God, I was only little, I didn't even know what the word sting meant.

"I want the medicine that stings," I said. *That sounds like the better one to me*, I thought in my own young mind. She smirked at my other aunt, and grandmother, and then said in her high pitched witchy poo voice, "Okay. The kind that stings it is." She filled the dropper with the medicine and then proceeded to pour the medicine onto the open cut on my knee. My knee began to sting and burn so terribly that I thought I was going to shoot through the roof. The pain was so intense that I jumped out of her arms and ran around in circles-into the bedroom, through the bathroom, out of the next bedroom, and through the kitchen. I was screaming and trying to run from the pain, but it followed me, I couldn't get away from it. My aunt stood there pointing and laughing hysterically at me. Finally the *nicer* one of my aunts (Tory) caught me as I was running and screaming. She picked me up and began to blow on my knee. I was now afraid of my aunt Hilda and didn't trust her anymore. If she hurt me once, she'll hurt me again- just because I look like my mother. I didn't understand what was wrong with that or why I was punished for it.

My mother tried her best to keep some normalcy in our dysfunctional life. She worked her fingers to the bone for us. She alone had the burden of providing for us girls, and contending with an extremely abusive and controlling husband-and had no support system what so ever. Life for my mother was an enormous struggle.

I am not making excuses for my mother (because there is no excuse) however, she had a very difficult childhood. She told me that her life was normal up until she was about 5-years-old.

CHAPTER SIX

MY NANA

My mother's mother (Nana) had the patients of a saint and was a wonderful mother. She stayed home to raise her four children; my mother, Raymond, Jimmy and Alfred. My grandfather, Raymond Sr., was a violinist in an orchestra. They played in most of the Block Island Hotels and nightclubs as well as around the tri-state areas. When my grandfather came home after touring one time, he got into an argument with Nana's brother, Alfred Sr. The argument became physical and Alfred Sr. grabbed a metal pipe and hit my grandfather in the head with it. My grandfather fell backward out of the third story window- smashing his head. He survived, but he had major brain damage and subsequently spent the rest of his life in a state institution. He didn't recognize any of his family members. He didn't even know his own name.

After my grandfather became incapacitated, Nana had to find work to feed and house her four young children. I couldn't begin to imagine how difficult this must have been for a woman in the 1940's. My Uncle Raymond, along with my mother tried to care for my Uncle Jimmy and baby Alfred. My mother was only-six-years-old.

A NICKEL IN MY SHOE

At the age of six months, my Uncle Alfred caught pneumonia and died. My mother said Nana began to drink heavily at that time. She started to frequent the neighborhood bar rooms, as well as bring strange men home. There often wasn't any food in the house, so they went hungry quite frequently. All of the children were left to fend for themselves. My mother said a man in a limousine stopped in front of her house while she and Uncle Jimmy were sitting on the front steps. The man tried to coax my mother (not my uncle) in to the car, telling her he had food and candy. My mother told him to go away or she would call her mama. The man told my mother that he *knew* her mama wasn't home. My mother said she grabbed my uncle and ran into the house. (*In later years, my Uncle Ray, before his own death in 2009, would lose two of his thirteen children to violence; Billy's throat was slashed while being robbed in a back alley in 1968, and Dennis was stabbed to death by his "best friend" in the early 70's, when he refused to hide a stolen car in his yard. My Uncle Jimmy's son was abducted in the late 60's. Because of this, he suffered many nervous breakdowns throughout his life. My uncle was on his way home from the hospital due to one such breakdown when he met his demise. It was the week of my honeymoon in 2006. My uncle stopped to help a drunken man stuck in the road, to change his flat rear tire. The man didn't realize my Uncle was still kneeling in back of the car. Instead of turning the car around, he put it in reverse in an attempt to drive backwards to the gas station that was 300 feet behind him, at the same time dragging my uncle to near death. He suffered with the entire left side of his body scraped to the bone for four hours, then succumbed to his injuries*).

I loved sleeping over Nana's house. She was a matronly looking woman, with short white hair and coke bottle glasses. I used to joke with her and tell her that she looked like the

MY NANA

cowardly lion from the Wizard of Oz movie. She was kind, and considered naïve. She lived in a crime-ridden part of Providence, and was mugged often by hoodlums. One time she got mugged and the mugger broke her arm when she wouldn't let go of her purse. Her arm was in a cast for the longest time.

I loved spending time with Nana, especially in the spring and summer seasons because she had a huge Lilac bush in her back yard. The wind would blow the flowery scent into her house. I loved that smell. She would let me pick the Lilacs, and then I would arrange them in a vase. I would place them in the middle of her kitchen table where everyone would be able to see my work of art.

I would scrub Nana's bathroom sink with Ajax for what felt like hours. I loved how she would tell me what a perfect job I did, and that her sink was the cleanest in the world. While I was in the bathroom cleaning the sink, she would come in and make me smoke the last third of her cigarette. She would tell me not to tell my mother. I didn't think I'd get in trouble any-way because everyone smoked. I remember going to the dentist and while he was examining me he had a cigarette dangling out of his mouth with a long ash at the end of it. I remember thinking if that ash falls in my mouth not only will it burn me, but I will vomit. Everyone smoked everywhere and anywhere; the grocery stores, hospitals, as well as in professional offices. Smoking advertisements plastered the billboards, television and, magazine covers, etc. It was actually strange to meet a non-smoker. Therefore, I didn't understand why it had to be kept a secret. Could it have been that I was only six-years old? Anyway, I never told my mother since Nana asked me not to.

As sweet, kind and gentle as Nana was during the day, she was equally as harsh and belligerent at night…after she began to drink. Her drink of choice was vodka and orange juice. She would swear and yell, mostly about how badly my mother treated Mary, Karen and I and how my Uncle Ray didn't do right by his children or wife.

Nana would take me to the bars (another secret) and tell everyone (loudly) I was her granddaughter and how pretty I was (very dangerous). I was both amazed and frightened at the same time- amazed because I got a glimpse in to the adult world, and frightened, because the adult world looked dark, depressing, and bleak. We would get tossed out of the bar room, and she would then pound on the bar room door while screaming obscenities. The bartender would, after a while, open the door long enough to tell her to leave or he would call the police on her. Then, it was off to the next drinking hole.

Nana was a devout Catholic. Her dream was for me to become a Nun when I grew up. She taught me how to say my prayers, and made me promise that I would say the Our Father and Hail Mary every night for the rest of my life before going to sleep. I promised. *(She also, when I was five, made me promise to name my first-born son Christopher after the Saint. I did.)*

Every Christmas and birthday she would give me religious gifts. One year she gave me a musical statue called, *"The Singing Nun."* I would wind it up and the Nun would spin around in circles, while the "Dominique" song played.

For my ninth birthday she gave me a crucifix with Jesus on it. She said it wouldn't bring me luck until a Catholic Priest blessed it with holy water. I asked my mother if I could spend the night at Nana's house so that we could go to church to have my cross blessed. She said yes, and then drove me to her house.

That night, Nana began to drink. After she was very intoxicated, she decided not to wait until tomorrow to have my cross blessed. She got the notion to have my cross blessed NOW. We left the house around midnight or so and walked down to the Church Rectory. She began to bang on the Rectory door- all the while hollering that her granddaughter needed to have her cross blessed.

Finally, after what seemed like an hour, the priest opened the door and began to scold her. She wouldn't take no for an answer, and continued to argue with him. Finally, he gave in to her demand. He only had two choices: bless my cross or call the police. He chose the easy way out and threw some holy water on my cross, made the sign of the cross, said Amen then slammed the door shut.

That satisfied Nana, so we began our journey home. She wanted to stop at the bars along the way but I lied and told her I was tired, and wanted to go back to her house to go to sleep. She complied.

CHAPTER SEVEN

JUST ME AND MOMMY

My mother never properly learned how to be a kind and loving mother because she never really had one herself. She told me she made a promise to herself early on in life and that was she would always have food in her house, (especially milk and butter) and her children would never go hungry. This was very commendable, and she had good intentions. However, being a good parent is so much more then just ensuring that your children don't go hungry.

Unfortunately, the bad times, without a doubt, outweighed the good times in my childhood, however, I do have some fond memories that I will treasure forever.

My mother would play the radio when she cleaned the house. The radio station we listened to was WPRO AM, with "Salty Brian in the morning." Oh how I love 60's music. I knew all the words to every song...Build Me Up Butter Cup... Crimson and Clover...Dizzy.... I love them to this day. My first records were the Jackson 5's *ABC*, the Archie's *Sugar, Sugar*, and The Partridge Family's (David Cassidy), *I Think I Love You*. The 45's came on back of cereal boxes. I would cut them off of the back of the box with scissors and play them on the record player. Music would almost always make me forget all the feelings of insecurity, pain and terror in my life, even if it was only for a short while. It was a much needed break from my pathetic reality.

On occasion my mother and father would take my sister's and I to the park where we would ride on the ponies have a picnic, or if it was snowing we would go sledding. My most fond memory of my mother was when she was up ironing one very hot night. We lived on the second floor in the city; we didn't even own a fan (did they even have fan's back in the mid 60's?) She ironed *everything*- sheets, underwear and even face cloths. It was so hot in my room one night that I woke up. I tossed and turned. I tried to go back to sleep but couldn't, the heat was unbearable.

I guessed it to be about 1:00 or 2:00 in the morning. I got up out of bed and came into the kitchen where my mother was finishing up with the last of the ironing. She was dripping with sweat.

I walked by her and sat at the kitchen table. I was anticipating getting sent back to bed. My mother didn't send me back to bed but what she did do next shocked me. She actually *spoke* to me, as if I was a *real human being*. "What's the matter, Sue, you can't sleep?" she asked. "No, Mommy," I replied. "It's too hot." What she said next shocked me even more.

"How about we take a walk down the street to the donut shop and get a Chocolate Cream donut, just you and me?"

Oh my God, I had all kinds of thoughts running through my mind, and felt an emotion that I have never felt before. I couldn't explain what I was feeling at my young age. All I knew is that I never felt this before, and I couldn't figure out what it was, or if there was even a name for it. (*It did have a name, what I was feeling was a sense of hope.*)

I remember feeling so excited that I thought I was going to jump out of my skin. I remember thinking, "just me and Mommy, she wants *me* to take a walk with her, and she wants to buy *me* my favorite donut. I feel so special." I must be dreaming because I don't feel afraid, my stomach isn't sick, and best of all my mother wants *me* to go with her, and she's not angry at me. *This* is what being in heaven must feel like.

At nearly 6-years-old, I remember this as being the very best day of my entire childhood. There wasn't one better before it, or after it. I have treasured that memory, tucked it away, and when I think of my mother, that's the day that I like to remember. Just her and I, walking, talking and eating a chocolate cream donut together-just the two of us in the middle of the night. The next day, however, would be very different.

CHAPTER EIGHT

A GOOD REASON TO CRY

It was just another day at Inter-City Elementary school. It sat in the heart of an old and broken down city, where the poorest of poor lived, or should I say existed. Poverty stricken-there weren't many people that lived there that didn't worry about where their next meal was coming from, but at least Terri Lyn isn't stealing *my* lunches anymore. She actually doesn't even bother me at all these days. I just don't understand it. I never do anything to her and she bullies me-I punch her in the face and she stops picking on me-doesn't make sense. Don't get me wrong, I'm not complaining!

After lunch, the school nurse came in to our classroom. She made all of us put our heads down on our desk. She ran her fingers through our hair, one by one. Sometimes, after running her fingers through someone's hair, she would write on the pad she carried with her, and sometimes she didn't, I thought this was strange.

I almost missed the bus today. I'm glad I didn't. I wanted to sit with my new friend "Calvin." Calvin just moved here, and I was lucky enough that he was placed in my class! I felt sorry for him. He looked so sad. He must have missed his friends, you know, moving to a new neighborhood and a new school. That's pretty tough on a kid.

I hope the bus driver doesn't catch me sneaking to sit with Calvin in the back of the bus today. That's where he and the rest of the colored people *had* to sit. (So much for desegregation, there was no such thing on my bus!)

I asked Calvin why he looked so sad. He said he was hungry all the time. He said there wasn't any food in his house because his mother didn't come home very often to buy any. "At least I have a mother at home *and* food in my house. Not much, but we have some." I thought to myself, "Wow, the only time my mother ever left my sisters and I was during the night to go to work. She worked the 11-7 shift in a jewelry factory, but we weren't alone. On the nights that my father didn't come home, Mrs. Lord, the lady who lived upstairs, would come down and sleep on the couch. The only time we were without supervision is when my mother slept during the day, after working all night.

I felt very sad for Calvin. I told him that I would share my school lunch with him everyday. That brought a smile to his face. "Hey," said Calvin, "Do you think you can come over and play at my house on Saturday?" I'll ask my mother, and if she allows me to go over to your house on Saturday I'll bring you some food, I told him. This is my stop. See you tomorrow, Calvin!

I was surprised to see my mother waiting for me on the front steps of our tenement house. It was a creepy house. It stood three stories high and had an apartment on each level. It was dark brown in color, and the style was old Victorian. It would have made a great haunted house at Halloween. It stood in a row with similar houses. Fortunately, our house was located closer to the top of the hill, because at the bottom there was the scariest thing-the graveyard. Most every night I would dream that all the dead people would rise from their graves and chase me, very slowly, almost zombie like. I would try to run from them but I ran even slower than they did. Right as the dead people were about to capture me I would float into my next dream. It usually had to do with water…deep dark water- a vast ocean, with huge tidal waves that would crash down on me. There was no way out of the water. Huge smooth rocks blocked the waters' edge. I would wake up in a cold sweat, and gasping for air.

My mother was standing there with her hands on her hips. She only struck that pose when she was irate. She looked mad! My mind started racing, trying frantically to think of what it was I did wrong. She grabbed me by the hair of my head and half dragged; half carried me up the stairs to our apartment.

She yelled at me over and over again, "You PIG! You filthy disgusting PIG! You have bugs in your hair!"

She dragged me by my hair through the kitchen and in to the pantry.

"I got a phone call from school today, you filthy pig. Strip all of your clothes off and climb on that chair."

As I stood there naked, she grabbed the scissors, picked up my hair so forcefully that I fell off the chair, she then proceeded to throw me back on to the chair by my hair. She continued to rant, non-stop.

"This is what you get for catching bugs," she said, and began to chop my hair off, whacking at it as if she were whacking her way through a forest with a machete. I didn't understand what I did wrong. *What were bugs?* I told her through screams and sobs that I was going to throw up. She said to me "if you fuckin' throw up you'll be eating it for supper! Now SHUT UP!"

My long hair was now scattered all over the pantry floor. She left me standing there on the chair. I was naked, cold, and so humiliated, but above all I was confused. I couldn't understand for the life of me what I did to deserve this violent haircut. While she was gone to (hopefully) get me some pajamas, I placed my hand on my head to feel the damage. Some parts of my head felt like skin, others felt like they had some hair. My bangs were totally gone, cut right up to my scalp. I was so afraid that my teachers, Shawn, Calvin and classmates were going to laugh at me, make fun of me and think I was ugly.

I heard my mother walking up the cellar steps. *What could she have needed from the basement?* That place was scary! Nobody ever went down there.

She walked in to the pantry and what she was carrying frightened me to my core. I started to feel dizzy and weak. I felt as though my knees were going to buckle, but I couldn't let that happen or there was no telling what she would do to me while I was laying on the floor. My head felt very numb and tingly. She was carrying a thick leather belt and a container of kerosene-*"oh my God, was she going to set me on fire?"*

"TURN AROUND!" she said through gritted teeth, in a loud, but monotone voice. I reluctantly began to turn around. I guess I didn't turn fast enough because she grabbed me by my neck and swung me around to face the sink. I was so cold and was utterly terrified. I remember turning my head to glance at both of my sisters. They were standing between the doorway of the kitchen and pantry. With her eyes and mouth wide open, Karen was looking on in horror and shock. Mary stood there watching- with a smirk on her face.

A GOOD REASON TO CRY

My mother turned the water on, but she ONLY turned on one side-the hot side. Soon there was steam coming from the sink. "Stick your head under the water," she demanded. "But Mommy it's too hot!" I cried. "DO IT NOW," she demanded as she wailed on my rear-end with the leather belt. I tried to stick my head under the scalding hot water. I screamed a blood-curdling scream and pulled my head out; WHAM…went the belt on the back of my legs. I could hear Karen screaming for her to stop whipping me. My mother continued to scream "GET YOUR HEAD UNDER THAT WATER NOW!" "I can't. It's too hot-it's burning me!" I cried. My mother grabbed me by the back of my neck and forced my head under the scalding hot water. I tried to fight. I tried to pull back as hard as I could.

I was no match for her strength. She held me by my neck and was holding my head under the burning hot water. The more I fought to pull my head out of the water, the faster and harder she whipped me with the belt, on my butt, and all over the back of my legs.

She grabbed the container of kerosene and began to dump it all over my head. It was splashing everywhere. It was pouring into my eyes. My eyes were burning, they felt as if they were on fire and about to explode. The burning liquid was running down my back to my private parts which began to sting and burn. It felt as if my entire body was on fire. "My eyes, I think I'm blind…I can't see!" I screamed. My mother proceeded to rip me off of the chair and drag me to my bedroom by what little hair I had left, and threw me onto the bed. I couldn't stop screaming-from the boiling water, the beating with the belt and the kerosene in my eyes, and private parts. Every inch of me was burning, from the top of my head to the soles of my feet. The louder I screamed and cried, the louder she would scream at me to shut up. She was so angry because I wouldn't stop crying.

"I'll give you a good reason to cry," she screamed through gritted teeth. My mother proceeded to grab me by my hair, turn my head, and pour the kerosene in my left ear. *Oh My God, if I don't die from pain now I never will*, I thought to myself. It burned so terribly. She held my head still so the kerosene would run deep into my ear canal. The pain in my ear was so intense that I began to slip in and out of consciousness. I was getting quieter. At this point, I was only able to sob. The pain was still just as intense but I could feel my self becoming thoroughly exhausted and weak. It felt as if I was drifting away. I would pass out, and then the intense pain would wake me up. *(I only remember thinking how grateful and relieved I was that she didn't set me on fire.)*

BANG BANG BANG BANG BANG...I heard someone pounding on the front door. I was lying there fantasizing that it was someone who came to rescue Karen and me, someone who would take us away from *her* forever.

It was only Mrs. Lord, the old lady who lived upstairs. She babysat for us at night sometimes, when my mother was away at work. She was mean and crotchety. If I had to guess her age, I'd guess it to be around 140-years-old or so. She was tall and skinny with blue/gray colored hair. Her skin was as wrinkled as a sun-dried raisin. She walked around with a large stick that she would use to hit her dog (King) when he didn't obey her commands. I didn't think Mrs. Lord liked me- until today. I didn't think anybody liked me. How could they when my own mother didn't even like me?

Mrs. Lord had to make us breakfast if my mother wasn't home from work in time to feed us before we had to leave for school. She would always make us oatmeal. She never put milk, sugar and butter in it like my mother did, even though we asked her to. The oatmeal was so thick that it would get caught in my throat. It felt as if my throat was being glued shut. The texture of it was so slimy that it made me gag and want to vomit.

One morning I refused to eat Mrs. Lords' oatmeal. "You best eat that on the double or yerr gonna be in a heap a trouble, young lady," she said with a twang.

"I can't Mrs. Lord," I replied. "It will make me throw up." Unexpectedly, she raised her hand and whacked me across the face so hard that I thought my head was going to go flying off of my shoulders. "Now you best do as I say." she said calmly, as if she didn't hit me in the face at all. After I stopped crying, I began to eat the oatmeal. I got to my third spoonful of the slimy goop and it wouldn't go down my throat. I made a mad dash to the bathroom and vomited.

My mother came walking through the door from work. She looked exhausted and pale. Mrs. Lord told her I was a bad girl because I wouldn't eat my oatmeal. My mother began to scold me in front of Mrs. Lord, and then sent me off to school. I think my mother reprimanded me to appease Mrs. Lord because my mother depended on her to baby-sit for my sister's and I when my father wasn't home, which was quite often. Mrs. Lord was the reason why my mother was able to work.

I heard one of my sister's open the door. Mrs. Lord came crashing through and ran in to my room, where my mother was standing over me by the bed. She grabbed my mother by her arm, dragging her out of my room and in to the kitchen.

"What are you doing to that baby!" Mrs. Lord hollered. "What is going on down here? I often hear a lot of yelling and banging going on in this house, but I have *never* heard a child scream like that before in my entire life! If I ever hear anything like that again, I will call the police."

Mrs. Lord stormed out of our house. I wanted to beg Mrs. Lord to call the police but I didn't have the strength or courage to speak. *(I can't remember if my mother participated in that conversation at all, I slipped in and out of consciousness, for what seemed like days).*

CHAPTER NINE

RATS IN THE CUPBOARD

While getting ready for school on my first day back from my horrible event, my mother made it very clear that if anyone asked what happened to my hair, I was to tell them that I cut it myself, and I was *stupid* for doing so.

I looked hideous. My mother gave me a kerchief to wear while my hair was growing out. The kerchief was probably more for her benefit then it was for mine. It hid the monstrous atrocity she had done to me.

I was very depressed after this. The kids in school poked fun at me everyday. They laughed and called me dumb and stupid for cutting my own hair. Calvin and Shawn were the only ones that didn't poke fun at me. Calvin even told me that I still looked pretty.

Calvin didn't come to school very often but when he did he looked disheveled and dirty. He smelled like urine and always complained he was hungry. He looked as if he was as sad as I was. I always shared my lunch with him on the days that he did come to school.

Calvin asked me to come to his house on Saturday. When I asked my mother, to my surprise, she said yes. But, she said I had to do my Saturday chores first, which consisted of dusting all the furniture and her knick-knacks. That took a very long time because if the chores weren't done to her liking, I had to start all over again.

I was so excited about going to Calvin's house to play on Saturday that I could hardly sleep on Friday night. I went to bed extra early so that I could wake up early, do all my chores, and walk to his house. He lived about four city blocks away from me on the main street. That wasn't too far to walk, I thought.

I finished my chores, to my mothers liking, and after lunch she let me walk to Calvin's house. I filled my pockets with little bags of crackers and cheese and began my journey.

I spotted a young (and very skinny) cat along the way. It was roaming around an old burned out house. I was always bringing stray animals home. I would tell my mother that the animals followed me home. The truth was that I carried them home. That's how we got Bridget. She was part Beagle, and something else. She was black and white with brown spots. I just found her and carried her home one-day. My mother said we could keep her. Our other dog, Mushy, (because she kissed us a lot), was a Collie and German Sheppard mix, with red and white fur. She had belonged to one of my uncles. My mother said that he fed her beer, and then beat her every night, so she took Mushy home to live with us. (How ironic).

I decided that, on my way home from Calvin's house, I was going to take that little cat home with me if I could catch it.

As I approached Calvin's house I could see him waiting for me in his front yard. He had his hands in his pockets, and as he was looking down he was kicking little rocks in a sweeping motion with one foot. He didn't look very happy at all, but when he saw me walking up the street a big smile came to his face. He asked if I had any food for him. I said yes, and pulled a bag of cheese out of my right pocket, a bag of crackers out of my left pocket and handed them to him. He gobbled up that food as if he hadn't eaten in a very long time.

"Is this *really* where you live?" I asked.

His house was a three-story tenement house; it had no paint on it, just bare wood. Some of the windows had been boarded, the rest were cracked. There was dirt where grass should have been, and the chain link fence in the front was rusted, warped, and had fallen down in various sections.

"Yup, come on in," he said.

We walked through the front door. It was cold, the air was still and it smelled like rotting meat. I couldn't believe what I saw. The inside of the house was empty and dirty. The only piece of furniture in the entire house was an old stained mattress that had been placed in the living room. The paint that once covered the walls had long since worn off, and the floors were worn to the bare wood. And no one could walk up stairs because most of the steps were missing.

"Come here," Calvin said. "I want to show you something."

I thought it was going to be something good because he had enthusiasm in his voice. We walked into the kitchen and he started opening up the cupboards. There were dead rats, of various sizes, in most all of them! I screamed and ran out of the house. I couldn't believe my eyes. I asked Calvin where his mother was. He said he didn't know and that she hadn't come home to see him in days. He said he had older brothers, but they hardly ever came home either.

A NICKEL IN MY SHOE

We didn't do much playing. We kicked some rocks around for a while, and took a walk around the block, that was about it. The sun was starting to go down, and I knew it was almost time for me to start walking home. I felt awful leaving him there all alone. I wanted to help him but I didn't know how. I said goodbye, and that I would see him Monday in school. I didn't know this would be the last time that I would see my best friend Calvin.

On my way home I spotted the little cat. He was hiding behind a section of broken lattice at the burned out house. I walked through the fence, bent down and started making kissing noises to him. I held out my hand as if I had food in it. The cat came running to me- meowing very loudly. I scooped him up in my arms and carried him home. I lied and told my mother that he had followed me home. She didn't fall for my scheme this time. I think she was catching on to me. I begged her to let me keep him, but my pleading fell on deaf ears. She opened a can of tuna and fed him. Then she loaded him in to the car and dropped him off at the pound.

While we were eating dinner that night I told my mother about Calvin's house; how there were dead rats in the kitchen cupboards, how he is always hungry, and his mother and brothers are never home. After dinner she made me take her to where he lived. I pointed his house out to her, and she stopped in front of it. I thought we were going to pick him up so he wouldn't have to be alone anymore. However, she retrieved a piece of paper and pen from her purse and began to write something down. She proceeded to turn the car around and we headed home. When we returned home from Calvin's house my mother called someone on the telephone. She was whispering so that I couldn't hear what she was saying.

RATS IN THE CUPBOARD

Monday was here already. I was looking forward to seeing Calvin. I was going to ask him to come over my house to play on Saturday but he never showed up for school...that day...or any day after. I was so sad. I never saw my friend again.

CHAPTER TEN

MIND GAMES

My home life pretty much remained the same except for the fact that my mother started to put her foot down with my father. She demanded that he find and maintain a steady job, as well as insisted that he stay away from the bar he frequented. When he wouldn't comply she would tell him to move out of the house. Mary, Karen and I would beg, plead and cry to my mother to let him move back in. My father would make lots of promises that he didn't intend to keep (or was incapable of keeping). Our tears and his empty promises worked a few times, but then he would resort to his old ways, and she would throw him out again. This cycle happened about three times, until one day my mother announced that they were getting divorced, and that we would soon be moving. This news devastated me.

My father seemed to easily accept the fact that their marriage was really over, too easily it seemed. It appeared as if he was tired of having a family- tired of being held down. He wanted to be free so he didn't put up any kind of a fight. He wasn't done playing his games though. He did stop physically harming her- for the time being, anyway. However, his psychological punishments were terrible.

A NICKEL IN MY SHOE

I thought that I was my fathers' favorite kid. He landed a job as a truck driver, and would pick me up from school every once in a while to ride on his truck with him. I felt so special. He was quiet as we rode, he didn't talk much at all. I sometimes wondered why he went out of his way to take me out of school to go to work with him if he had nothing to say to me. I didn't really care. As long as I was with him I was happy.

My father would drop me off in front of the house when he was finished with work. He would have a huge smile on his face. I thought it was because he was happy that I came to work with him, and that he loved me and missed me.

When I entered my house my mother would begin to yell at me. I didn't understand why she was so angry. She was angry not so much at me, but at my father. She would then call him at my grandmothers' house where he was living, and, very loudly ask him why he took me without telling her. She told him how worried she was, and how he better not do that again, or she would call the police.

He did the same thing with Karen- only my mother took Karen's 'disappearance' much harder. My father signed her out of school one day, and when she didn't come home from the bus stop my mother panicked. She was running up and down the streets screaming my sisters' name, and crying. My father had that same smile on his face when he pulled up in his truck to drop my sister off- my mother cried while hugging and clinging on to her. I didn't understand what was going on at the time. However, I see clearly now that my father used me to hurt my mother, and when taking me only made her angry, he took my sister- and received the reaction he was looking for- devastation and fright. He hurt her in one of the most terrible ways possible.

MIND GAMES

My father soon shacked up with someone that he met at the bar. We wouldn't see him for weeks, and sometimes months on end. Sure, he told us that he was going to pick us up every Sunday, but he never did. Mary, Karen and I waited on the stairs every week. He disappointed us week after week.

After waiting all day on the front steps of the house, I would call him at the bar he frequented. "Is Bobby there?" I would ask. I would hear a voice in the background say, "tell her I'm not here." *(I didn't want to believe that it was my father's voice.)* "O.k., please tell him to call his daughter Susan when he gets there," I would say. I then began my vigil by the telephone, but the return phone call from my father never came.

Mary finally smartened up and stopped waiting for my father, unlike Karen and I. We continued to wait for him every Sunday on the front stairs. We waited from the minute we woke up until it got dark out, and then we waited by the phone until it was time for us to go to bed. We would lay there awake, still hoping for the phone to ring. It never did.

I missed, and longed for my father immensely. I felt so lost and vulnerable without him. It made my mother angry to watch us girls wait from sun up to sun down, every weekend for our father to pick us up, knowing all the while that he had no intention of keeping his promise to us. My mother tried to tell us he wasn't going to pick us up, but we didn't want to believe her. We would say, "yes he is Ma, he'll show up." She was right, he hardly ever did.

My mother, Mary, Karen and I moved to Orland Beach in the summer of 1970. I was nine years old. We moved into a Cape Cod style, single-family house. It was a real home. It was cozy with a fireplace in the living room, and it sat only a few yards away from the ocean. It was a beachfront community that never attracted a higher class of people, like you'd expect an ocean community would. The neighborhood may as well have been filled with old, broken down trailer homes because that is what most of the people lived like. They had a backwoods type mentality, where children were to be seen and not heard, as well as placing little value on children's feelings or lives.

It appeared as if the majority of the people in the neighborhood were disheveled, dirty and very poor. It was a mostly a white neighborhood, which seemed strange to me because I was accustomed to being the minority. They also didn't speak proper English, which made them sound very ignorant and uneducated. They used the word *ain't (meaning 'am not')* a lot in their sentences, as well as the word *yous* (meaning 'you two').

There were many changes taking place in all of our lives at this particular time. My mother considered the neighborhood to be safer than the one we moved from, and we all were getting older, therefore she gave us a little more freedom. Mary met a gang of kids who were into taking drugs and skipping school. She started to get in to a lot of trouble in those two areas. They would all hang out and get high at the carrousel, which was located at the top of the street that lead to the beach. This was Mary's favorite place in the world. She finally found people and a place where she felt she belonged. She started to stay out all night long with her friends. I can't say that I minded because her focus was off of hurting me, at least most of the time.

Mary's behavior got to be so self-destructive that my mother took her to a Psychiatrist for an evaluation. She was soon diagnosed as having Schizophrenia. This is somewhat rare for a person of her age. We always knew Mary had a mental problem, and now it had a name. *(If I had to take an educated guess, I'd say*

MIND GAMES

she had a touch of Asperger's Syndrome as well; the most mild, and high functioning form of Autism)

Mary was placed on a drug called Lithium. It didn't seem to help her at all. In my opinion it made her behavior worse. Not only was she taking lithium, but she was taking illegal drugs with her friends as well. Mary became too much for my mother to handle. Her behavior was more violent then ever, and she said the voices in her head told her to do bad things. The last straw was when Mary stole my mother's car in the middle of the night and totaled it. My mother became desperate and asked my father to come and live with us in our new home.

After moving in, my father, once again, made promises that he wasn't able to keep. He stayed away from the bars for about a week then he was back to his old ways. This time he was doing much more than drinking. He was taking drugs. I found little brown vials on the kitchen table one night. My mother was mortified. They fought about his new substance problem alot. Soon he was back to all of his old ways plus a couple of new ones. My mother asked him to move out, and he did.

I don't think my mother thought it through when she asked my father to move in with us. She thought she needed him in order to control Mary's behavior, she didn't stop to think about who was going to control *his* behavior.

One night, after we all went to bed, I heard noises coming from downstairs. It sounded if someone was trying to break in through both our front window and then through our front door. I had just drifted off to sleep, therefore thought I was only hearing things or maybe dreaming. Soon after that, I woke up to Mary lying beside me. I heard the sound of my mother screaming and crying, "Bobby, stop...help...someone help...Mary...Sue...help! When I attempted to jump out of the bed Mary grabbed me and held me down.

"You're not going anywhere," she said. "That bitch deserves what she is getting."

I didn't understand. She was denying help for my mother. Someone was hurting her, I wanted to help her. I wanted to get to the phone to call the police but my sister restrained me and told me to "shut up and listen." I listened to my mothers screams and cries for help for what felt like hours. I couldn't comprehend why Mary didn't want to call the police. Wasn't she, at the very least, afraid that the person who was hurting my mother would come and hurt us next? I didn't understand why she wasn't afraid.

When I awoke the next day, Mary wasn't beside me in bed. I dashed out of bed and ran to my mother's room. There was a heavy metal frying pan lying on the floor beside her bed. Both of her eyes were black and blue right down to her cheekbones, and her eyes were swollen shut. She was unrecognizable. I started to cry and tell her I was sorry for not being able to help her. She said my father broke into the house and beat her in the head with the frying pan and that she couldn't see. She told me to call the rescue.

Mary stood in the doorway with the most evil look on her face. My mother asked her if she let my father in when we were sleeping. Mary never answered. She smirked and walked away. I didn't want to believe my father was capable of doing something that vicious to my mother or that my sister was in on it. My mother *must have* been mistaken.

I called the police and the rescue for my mother. The police questioned us. I told them what I heard, but didn't dare tell them Mary held me down. Karen slept through it all, and

MIND GAMES

Mary lied. She told them she was sleeping and didn't hear a thing.

The EMT's were busy examining my mother. She refused to go to the hospital because she didn't have anyone to leave us with. She didn't dare leave us alone with Mary. They told her if her eyesight didn't come back in a few days, or if she started to vomit, she would have to go to the hospital or her doctor.

My mother called me in to her room after they left. She asked me if I heard her screaming my name. I told her I was afraid to tell her the truth. She assured me not to be afraid, that she wouldn't be mad. I told her that I wasn't afraid of her, that I was afraid of Mary. She said no matter what I told her that she would not tell Mary. I began to tell her that I heard her screaming and tried to get out of bed to come and help her, but Mary held me down- telling me that you deserved what you were getting. *(My mother broke her promise- while beating Mary, my mother blurted out what I had told her. I paid the price one Saturday while my mother was away. Mary chased me around the neighborhood for hours- giving me a beating every time she caught me. She would then let me go, chase me, catch me and beat me again. This went on until my mother arrived home that evening.)*

I think my mother was in denial up until that point. She finally realized exactly how serious Mary's mental problems really were and that my sister lacked a conscience. She also recognized that Mary was malevolent, dangerous, and capable of just about anything, including murder.

My mother kicked her out of the house at the ripe old age of thirteen. Mary went from my father's (and grandmothers) to my aunts and friends houses. When she did or said something that would scare any one of them, they would toss her out on the street and on to the next house she would go.

CHAPTER ELEVEN

CAT O' NINE TAILS

As for me, I would hang out with the Connor kids. They lived in back of us on the adjacent street. There were nine kids in their family, and ranged in age from three months to twelve-years-old.

I remember the first time I was invited into their house- it was late afternoon. I was standing in the living room waiting for one of the kids to come back downstairs when I noticed a woman sleeping on the couch and I heard a baby crying. I couldn't tell where the sound was coming from. I followed the echo of the crying over to near the couch area but I didn't see a baby. I walked closer to the couch. What I saw shocked me. A little baby girl was stuck down in-between the couch cushions. I picked her up and cuddled her.

The way they treated this baby was appalling. The kids would toss her high in the air and catch her. I held my breath and begged them to stop. They laughed at me, and only did it more- just to get my reaction. When it came time for feeding, they didn't spoon feed her. They would dump a jar of what ever baby food that was available into a bottle with a large hole cut in the top of the nipple. It would pour all over her and she would choke. Certainly, more food landed on her clothing than in her belly. I went over everyday after that just to make sure she was taken care of-even if I had to do it myself.

I thought my mother was cruel until I met *their* parents. Their punishments were vicious and sadistic. Mr. and Mrs. Connor would wake the four oldest kids up in the middle of the night, place piles of rice on the metal strip that separated the floor in the kitchen from the carpet in the living room. The children would then be forced to kneel on the rice for hours while holding their arms straight out in front of them. If they let their arms move or fall, their mother would whip them with a leather belt.

Mrs. Connor would first order her children to change into long sleeved shirts and pants. They were then forced to kneel in front of her so that she could whip them with a belt called the *cat o' nine tails*. Mrs. Connor would accuse them of doing bad things that they really didn't do, such as accusing the girls of having sex with boys. The girls would adamantly deny the accusations while getting beat. She would force them, through whipping them, to confess. When they couldn't stand the pain and suffering any longer they would finally tell their mother what she wanted to hear-hoping it would make her stop. But the confession always backfired on them- she would torture them all the more because of the 'crime' they admitted to.

I can recall the day their stepfather brought, what they called the cat *o' nine tails* home. That thing was scary look-ing! It had multiple, thin leather strips hanging off of it. Mrs. Connor was *so* excited- she acted as if she had just received a new toy. The four oldest children got whipped that day with the new belt while their mother and stepfather laughed. She made them watch each other get whipped, one by one, so that the next child in line would be well aware of his/her fate. She loved to see the expressions of terror in their eyes and on their faces. She thoroughly enjoyed inflicting pain and suffering on her children.

They hardly ever went to school, but when they did the teacher would call Mrs. Connor on the phone to say that a particular child was falling asleep in class. She neglected to tell the teacher it was because they were either forced to go without sleep all night, or they went to bed late, and then were ripped from a sound sleep soon after to receive a punishment of some kind. When that child came home from school there was hell to pay.

In order to eat, they had to wait until their mother was asleep so they could sneak food. If they were caught they got punished. This was another of her sadistic games.

They didn't get whipped, deprived of sleep or starved because they did anything wrong. They received these punishments because their mother derived pleasure from it. There was one child that Mrs. Connor picked on the most. She was a little younger than me, maybe about 7 or 8-years-old. I remember when Mr. Connor came home with a box of clothes from the Salvation Army. She forced her to try on a size 2-toddler shirt. Obviously, the shirt got stuck on her head and arms while she was struggling to get in to it. The shirt acted as a straight jacket. While she was stuck in this shirt, her mother began to whip her all over her body, and was screaming at her to "put it on...put it on...hurry up you little fuck...!" This is what her mother repeated to her over and over again. It was so sickening to watch that I left the house and ran home.

By now I became immune to their mother's abusive behavior. I never felt that she would hurt me. In fact, I got the feeling that she liked me. Believe it or not, this woman and her husband would be my savior one day.

CHAPTER TWELVE

FOR THE LOVE OF A MAN

Karen was busy making friends of her own in the neighborhood. Because we were getting older, she and I began to separate, and become a little bit more independent of each other. She had her set of friends and I had mine. Never the less I continued to be very protective of her.

We continued to wait for my father to pick us up every week. He managed to show up every once in a blue moon with a different girlfriend on his arm every time. He had many girlfriends, but I remember two in particular.

The first one's name was Sharon. She was pretty with shoulder length brown hair. Sharon had a newborn baby girl that unfortunately, she thoroughly neglected.

My father picked Karen and I up one Sunday and brought us back to Sharon's house. She was a stripper in a men's club and was getting ready for work as the baby lay crying in a play-pen. I asked if I could pick the baby up and she said, "I don't *care,*" and proceeded to walk out the front door.

I noticed, after picking the baby up, that she smelled horribly of feces and urine. Her diaper was overflowing with it and her gown was sopping wet from the excrement. She also had black tarry like goop all around the creases in her neck and crust all over her scalp. Her mouth was making frantic suck-ing gestures, and she was trying desperately to eat her fists. My father didn't even seem to care. He just continued to watch the football game on TV. This infant was utterly neglected.

The baby was shivering either from the wetness of her cloth-ing, hypoglycemia, or maybe both. She was so wet I couldn't hold her. I began to prepare a bath for her. I couldn't find baby soap or lotion so I smelled the adult soaps and bottles of lotion that were in the bathroom and tried to pick which ones would be the most gentle on baby skin. I found a diaper and a t-shirt along with a clean gown and socks. I couldn't find a clean blan-ket so I borrowed one of my fathers flannel shirts. I felt the water. It was warm to the touch. I placed the baby into the tub and began to wash her. I started at her head, trying gently, with a face cloth, to remove some of the scales that were caked on her scalp. I washed her body twice, especially her neck. Her poor private areas were red and raw. I soaked her little bum for a few minutes but she was screaming, not because of the bath but because of hunger. I didn't soak her bottom for too long because I was afraid my father would get mad and aggravated because of her crying. (*God forbid if anyone was to make a peep during a football game!*) I removed her from the tub, placed her in a towel and dried her off. I looked through all of the cabinets in the bathroom and found Vaseline to put on the baby's bot-tom. Then, I got her dressed, wrapped her in the flannel shirt, warmed a bottle of formula and fed her. She drank so fast that she choked periodically. She vomited soon after she was finished eating. I changed her and fed her again, and then I rocked her to sleep. This is what I would do with the Connor baby and my Thumbelina dolls, so I considered myself fairly experienced for an eleven year-old. I worried about and cried for that poor little baby everyday.

Soon after that day, the baby was taken away from Sharon, thank God. She didn't seem to mind that her baby was gone. *All* she cared about was my father, and making *him* happy.

On the next visit with my father and Sharon, she decided to take all of us shopping for clothes at the Mall. I thought it was strange that she walked in with a baby carriage; after all she didn't have a baby anymore. She told me to pick out an outfit. I picked out a tennis outfit. I didn't play tennis. I just thought it was cute. She took it from me and placed it in her baby carriage. My father also picked something out, so did Karen. What I didn't realize is that she never stopped at the register to pay for the items. She filled the baby carriage and walked out the front door of the mall. Needless to say, this was the last time we ever saw Sharon again. She was arrested for shoplifting soon after that, and my father found a new girlfriend to shack up with. Her name was Leigha. *(My father told me that after being released from jail, Sharon moved away to Florida where she committed suicide because he wouldn't take her back)*

CHAPTER THIRTEEN

DEVIL IN DISGUISE

My mother began to go out with her girlfriends more frequently. She was very discrete when it came to men and never brought any of the men home that she dated- unless she felt as if the relationship was going somewhere. My mother kept that part of her life separate and secret from us girls. One day my mother announced that she had a boyfriend and that she was bringing him home to meet us. I had mixed emotions about this. I felt as if I was about to betray my father, whom I haven't seen in weeks, however, I kept my thoughts and feelings to myself, because this is the happiest that I've ever seen my mother. In turn, she hit me less.

When I heard the doorbell ring, my mother said, "That must be Joel." She opened the door and a tall man stepped in. He looked to be at least twenty years her senior. He had salt and pepper colored hair. I could sense an air about him. She introduced us. He seemed nice enough, and he sure did smell nice too.

He told us that he was taking us to dinner, and asked if we have ever had Chinese food. Karen and I shook our head no. We proceeded to get into his car. It was big, white and fancy.

A NICKEL IN MY SHOE

Karen and I were excited. Not only have we never been out to eat in a fine restaurant before, but we have never ridden in a nice car before either. Karen climbed into the back seat first, and then I climbed in after her. We didn't get far up the road when my mother asked "what is that smell?" A foul aroma began to fill the air. Someone stepped in dog doo, I said. We all began to check our feet to find that it was Karen who stepped in it before entering the car. It was all over the carpet in the backseat of the car. My mother was embarrassed. I thought it was absolutely hilarious, but I was too afraid to laugh. It didn't appear to faze Joel at all. He pulled the car over to the side of the road, took out some towels and began an attempt to clean it up. He acted as if it was no big deal. This surprised me considering he acted and looked so clean, neat and perfect.

I was in amazement as we pulled into the parking lot of the restaurant. There were two huge lions, one on either side of the entrance. The decorations inside were fantastic. The waitress brought us over little fans to play with and asked what we would like to drink. Joel asked if he could order for us because he knew a special drink just for special little girls. Of course Karen and I said yes. He ordered two Shirley Temples. The drinks soon arrived. They were beautiful. The color was clear at the top and red at the bottom. They were adorned with an umbrella, and a string of cherries, not to mention they tasted delicious. When the waitress returned, Joel placed our order.

"We'll have a poo poo platter for four with a side order of fried rice, crab rangoon's, and beef sticks," he said. I was so afraid I wouldn't like any of this new, strange food and that I would be forced to eat it. I began to feel nervous.

First to arrive was the poo poo platter. I was amazed when I saw it. The food was situated around a Lazy Susan type tray with fire coming out of the bowl in the middle. It was so beautiful, and all the food tasted so delicious! I don't think I have ever enjoyed a meal more in my life, before or since.

After dinner, Joel announced that he was going to take us to a special place. Karen's and my excitement was building as we drove. The anticipation was almost too much to bear. He pulled into a parking lot of a toy store. It was closed. I asked what we were doing here.

"I own this store," he said. "You girls can have anything that you want in there."

"Anything?" I asked.

"Anything," he replied.

I pointed out to him that the store was closed, and he said he would turn off the alarm so we could enter. After fooling around with the alarm for a while we went in. Karen and I were thrilled. We walked up and down the isles trying to decide what toy we were going to pick out. We were eyeing the bikes because neither one of us have ever had one. The police soon came because he didn't properly deactivate the alarm. He had to prove ownership of the store. While Joel was busy with the police officers, my mother pulled us aside. She gave us strict instructions NOT to pick out a toy, but we were to thank Joel politely and tell him no thank you. I felt my heart sink. This was a once in a lifetime opportunity, and my mother had to mess it up for us. *(I felt at the time she didn't allow us to choose a toy out of meanness, however, now I realize it was out of pride.)*

My mother dated Joel for the next year or so. During that time, he became more comfortable and less pleasant to my mother and us girl's. He would tell her that Karen and I were slobs, and that we should be taught how to become neat like him. He would encourage her to *test* us. He instructed her to leave a sock in the middle of the staircase before they went out on their date. If it was still there when she came home, it indicated that we walked by it several times without picking it up. He then suggested that, as punishment, she was to wake us up when she returned home, empty all the drawers in the bedrooms, and we were to fold each and every piece of clothing, ever so neatly, and place it back in the drawers. That's exactly what she did. However, we received a beating first. My mother would rip us from our bed, out of a sound sleep and beat us with the belt. She would then dump all the drawers out, while screaming at us about what slobs we were.

Joel encouraged my mother to do the same thing with the dishes, silverware, pots and pans. If she came home and found as much as a spoon in the sink, she would wake us out of a sound sleep and beat us with the belt. She would proceed to empty all the dishes, silverware, pots and pans out of all the cupboards and we had to wash, dry and put them all away perfectly. If it wasn't done 'right', we had to start all over again- it took hours.

This went on every weekend for several months. When Joel began to pick on *her* for not being perfectly neat, the trouble in their relationship began. They argued a lot about it. They eventually broke up because of his fanatical behavior. I certainly didn't shed any tears! My mother was soon back in the dating scene.

CHAPTER FOURTEEN

THE TURNING POINT

One day, my mother announced she was going on a double date. She told me that I had to baby sit for her girlfriend Sara's son, and that I had to take Karen with me. For some reason I didn't want Karen to come with me. I had a bad feeling that day, and I didn't know why. But I knew that she certainly couldn't stay home alone.

My mother drove my sister and I over to her house. We walked in and her friend Sara introduced us to her two-year-old son. He was cute, with blonde hair and green eyes. After introducing us, she put him in his crib for the night. She showed us where the snacks and drinks, as well as where the diapers and bottles were. She told us to help ourselves to anything we wanted, and to sleep in her bed if we became tired. Then, they both left for the evening.

My mother always taught us that when we go on a babysitting job we should clean the house, and boy did this house need cleaning! There were clothes, toys, and junk thrown everywhere. The sink was piled sky high with dirty dishes and the bathroom was not only a mess but had a terrible stench as well.

A NICKEL IN MY SHOE

Karen and I went straight to work. She picked up all of the toys, clothes and junk that was scattered all over the floor. Karen also dusted all the furniture, straightened out all of the pillows on the couch, and vacuumed the carpets. I washed all the dishes, counters, and cleaned the bathroom. It looked, and smelled like a new house when we were finished. I was very proud of our work. If there's one thing my mother taught us, it was how to clean a house.

Karen and I watched television for a while. We were both fairly tired after all of the cleaning we did, and decided to change into our nightclothes and go to bed. The bedroom was big. I noticed a five-drawer dresser to the left as I walked through the bedroom door. The bed was to the right, and in front of the bed was a long dresser with a fancy mirror attached. Karen climbed into the bed on the side nearest the door. I checked on the baby, and locked the front door before climbing into the bed next to Karen. We were exhausted and fell asleep fairly quickly.

Then, at some time in the middle of the night, I felt hands creeping up my nightgown. I thought I was having a nightmare. I woke up kicking the hands away. It was pitch black in the room, therefore, I couldn't see a thing. That bad dream gave me the creeps, so I got up and stumbled my way to the living room where I sat on the couch trying to get my bearings.

A few minutes later I hear, "Susan, help me…help me!" It was Karen. *What was wrong?* I thought. I got up and went running to the bedroom; on the way by I turned on the bathroom light. The bathroom was next to the bedroom and I knew the light would shine in enough so I would be able to see, and not trip and fall.

When I ran in I saw two figures. I couldn't believe my eyes. A man was on top of my sister! I now realized that it wasn't a dream. Karen was screaming and crying.

THE TURNING POINT

"Get him off of me, Susan. He's heavy. He's hurting me."
I tried grabbing Karen's arm to pull her out from underneath
him, but he had her pinned tight. I was screaming for him to
get off of her. I began frantically looking around the dimly lit
room for a weapon to hurt him with. I turned around to look
on top of the five-drawer dresser that was in back of me, to see
if there was an object that was heavy enough to hit him with.
I spotted the telephone- it was the old-fashioned dial kind. It
had the coil that attached from the phone to the receiver. I
picked it up and began to smash him as hard as I could in the
back of his head with the receiver end of the phone. He began
to get weak, at which point I grabbed Karen's arm and began
to pull her out from under him. I was yanking on her arm so
hard I thought I was going to break it. She finally fell on to the
floor. I maintained a hold of her arm and dragged her out of
the bedroom and in to the kitchen. Then, I grabbed the phone
that was attached to the wall and dialed my home number. My
mother answered (thank God!), but I was crying and sobbing so
much that she couldn't understand what I was saying.

The drunken man came stumbling out of the bedroom,
clad only in his underwear. He grabbed the phone out of my
hand and hung it up. The phone immediately began, and continued to ring. He wouldn't let me answer it. He struggled
to maintain his balance. He started to stumble toward me so
that he could pin me up against the wall. I quickly grabbed
Karen and pulled her behind me. He began telling us not to be
afraid. He attempted to reach his arm around me in an effort to
touch or grab Karen, but I slapped his hand away and screamed
at him "keep your filthy hands off of my sister!" I could feel
Karen shaking. She was crying and sobbing. She kept repeat-
ing, "Oh, Susan, I'm so scared. I'm so scared." I told her it

would be all right, while maintaining eye contact with him. But I didn't believe my own words. I was terrified- thinking that he was going to rape and kill us. He would have to kill me first though, in order to get to Karen.

He was right up in my face, and reeked of alcohol. He told us that he thought we were his wife, (what he said didn't even make sense) slurring his words. He continued to mumble incoherently.

My mother, Sara, and my mother's date came running in with two police officers. It felt as if it took forever for them to get there. One of the police officers made Karen and I sit on the couch, while the other officer was questioning Sara's husband. All I could do the entire time I sat there was stare at that nasty green carpet. *(For many years the color green, as well as any man with blonde hair and blue eyes would make me nauseated)* I was so ashamed that I couldn't look him, or anybody else, in the eyes. He asked Karen and me if that man *(who happened to be Sara's husband- she was cheating on him that evening with another man.)* hurt us, or touched us in any inappropriate places. Karen and I looked at each other. We were so embarrassed. Karen and I shook our heads no. The police officer knew we were lying. He asked my mother if she wanted to press charges. My mother said no, she did not want to press charges. I was shocked! How could she allow this man to go unpunished for molesting her two young daughters? What kind of a mother would permit a man, who violated her children, get away scot-free? I couldn't wrap my mind around it. I always thought my mother didn't love me, this incident confirmed it.

New feelings and emotions were swiftly emerging. My feeling of fear was replaced by anger. Any feeling of love I had for her was replaced with hate. I felt dirty, worthless and ashamed. I started to become rebellious. I highly resented my mother for allowing that man to get away with violating us. She expected Karen and I to forget about it as if it never happened. My mother went as far as to let Sara and her son move in with us after that incident.

Sara was a slob! She slept all day and let her kid run wild. She allowed her son to tear the house apart. When we came home from school everyday, we walked in to a disaster area. Dishes were piled up in the sink, toys and dirty clothes were everywhere, cupboard doors were open, the counters tops were full of bottles with sour milk dried in the bottom of them and the laundry baskets were overflowing with dirty diapers. The bathroom was filthy with makeup everywhere, and she never flushed the toilet, so it smelled to high heaven! The house was a disaster and smelled worse then a sewer! First of all, I couldn't believe that my mother would let her live with us after what her husband had done to Karen and I. But to be forced to clean up after, and take beatings for the messes and filth that her and her son created was going too far. At first, if my mother came home and we hadn't cleaned the house she would beat us, while Sara looked on- emotionless and expressionless- full well knowing we were being beat for the mess she and her son made.

My mother was a clean and neat person and couldn't stand the mess and filth that this woman and her kid created on a daily basis. She wasn't comfortable asking that woman to clean up after herself and her son, so my mother took her frustrations out on us instead. That was the easiest and most cowardly way for her to relieve her stress- this was a perfect example of displaced anger.

I was eleven years old at this particular time. My feelings toward this woman were of resentment and hate. Therefore, we got into a heated argument and I proceeded to tell her *exactly* what I thought of her and her son—that she is a slob, and that I am not cleaning up after her anymore, as well as refuse to take beatings for a mess I didn't even make. I also screamed at her that I resented being punished for her mistake-marrying a pervert.

My mother walked into the house at that point. All three of us began to argue. My mother started to hit me, but I didn't cower. For the first time, I stood my ground and continued to speak my mind. I told her that I was sick of her, hated her and that I was going to live with my father. She screamed at me, "GO THEN, you both deserve each other."

I called my father at the bar room. After asking to speak with him, I told the man who answered the phone that I knew my father was there and not to lie to me. I demanded that he put my father on the phone. My father came to the phone. I was crying and told him that I needed to come live with him and Leigha because I couldn't tolerate living with my mother or her slob of a friend anymore. *(I didn't dare tell him that Sara's husband molested us. It was extremely embarrassing for me, and I somehow felt as if it was my fault. I buried it deep down inside of me and locked it away.)*

I asked him where Mary was living because I didn't want to live anywhere that she was. He said he didn't know where she was living or whom she was living with.

It took some begging and pleading before my father agreed to let me come and live with him and Leigha. He told me he would be by to pick me up later on in the evening. I stormed upstairs to my bedroom and began to pack my clothes. I started to think of Karen, and realized how much I was going to miss her. I began to regret my decision to leave. However, I couldn't stand my mother anymore. I completely despised her!

CHAPTER FIFTEEN

MUSTARD IN THE FRIDGE

I had just finished sixth grade. I didn't know then that would be my last formal year of school.

Living with my father and Leigha was like living alone. They were hardly ever home and there was barely ever any food in the apartment. Leigha had an eight-year-old son that slept in *his* bedroom, when he visited her every other weekend, therefore I didn't have a bedroom of my own. I had to sleep on the couch, even when he stayed with his Dad. Leigha made it clear that I shouldn't feel too comfortable there, and that I was merely a guest. My father would fall asleep on the couch while watching TV- therefore I had to sleep on the floor (even though there was an empty bed in the house). This happened quite often.

Summer was almost over and it was getting to be time for my father to register me in my new school. He continually made up excuses not to enroll me. He was merely being lazy and irresponsible. Finally, the day before school was to begin, he reluctantly took me to get registered. I was excited because I was going into junior high school and nervous because I wouldn't know anyone there.

A NICKEL IN MY SHOE

Once enrolled, I asked my father if he was going to buy me some new school clothes. Everyone loved to show off their new outfits on the first day of school. He said no because he didn't have any money. I was getting used to *that* answer. I only had two short-sleeved shirts and two pairs of jeans that barely fit me. I was very skinny to begin with, and I had lost more weight over the summer. However, I grew a couple of inches taller, and the majority of my old clothes didn't fit me anymore. My pants were too short, and my shirts were too big. By now, I was dreading school. I only had faded old clothes to wear that, for the most part, didn't even fit me. Since I didn't own a coat, I had to wear my father's flannel shirt in place of one. I guess I was lucky that my old sneakers still fit me.

I was utterly confused on my first day of school due to missing the orientation for new students. This orientation would have allowed me to explore, and become familiar with the layout of the school, as well as give me the opportunity to locate where each of my classes were. The school was so large that it actually looked more like a college. I went to the office to pick up my class schedule, and was ten minutes late for my first class. When I walked in, the kids looked at me and began to laugh. They all turned their heads to whisper to the kid sitting next to them. I tried to choke back the tears. When I found an empty seat, I sat there the entire time with my head down. I felt as if everyone was better than me. I felt "less than," and I was so embarrassed.

I made it to my second class, again about ten minutes late. I decided not to go in and made no attempt to find any more of my classes that day. Everyone else seemed to know where to go, except for me. I felt so lost, alone and humiliated.

MUSTARD IN THE FRIDGE

My father left the house to go on a drinking binge that night. I decided that I wasn't going to put myself through that agony and embarrassment again so I didn't attend school that week, or the following weeks for that matter. No one noticed, because no one cared—not the school, and certainly not my father. Besides, it was getting too cold to go outside without a *real* coat. The flannel shirt no longer sufficed.

I attended school every once in a great while. But when the snow started to fall, and the extreme cold got to be too much for me to tolerate, I didn't go to school at all.

There was hardly ever any food in the house. Leigha was responsible for paying the rent and all of the bills, as well as buying food for us because my father never worked. There also wasn't any soap, shampoo, or toothpaste in the house- Leigha's responsibility as well. Therefore I had numerous toothaches and large (embarrassing) sores on my face from not being able to brush my teeth or bathe.

Leigha was short; around five feet tall, petite, with long bleached blond hair. She didn't act dumb like my fathers' previous girlfriends. She seemed educated and certainly didn't belong with my father. Her son stopped coming to stay with us every other weekend, and soon Leigha stopped coming home. I didn't know exactly why, but I would guess that she was getting tired of supporting my father and me. I had no idea where she stayed when she was gone- but what I did know is that I missed her. Without Leigha there I knew I would starve.

The only food in the house was a jar of mustard in the fridge. I was so hungry that my stomach was burning- my stomach felt as if it was *eating itself*. I would open the food cupboard and fridge door several times a day- hoping food would *magically* appear.

A NICKEL IN MY SHOE

I was becoming very scared. I didn't know how much longer I could survive without eating. I was so famished that I could barely think straight. I was becoming extremely desperate-trying to think of ways to get food.

CHAPTER SIXTEEN

CHEAT TO EAT

Leigha had been gone for what felt like forever, and my father and I were stuck in the apartment due to a snowstorm. Also, he didn't own a car. I was so desperate for something to eat that I asked my father if he wanted to play a game of Gin Rummy with me for money. I had already planned on cheating to win, knowing full well the very likely consequence-a brutal beating. I was *so* hungry that I was willing to take that chance.

He said if I won he would give me five bucks. I agreed and dealt the cards. I blatantly cheated, he had to have noticed. However, I was determined to win no matter what. It was my only chance to get food. I didn't care if he hit me for winning; I desperately needed something to eat.

I won the game. To my amazement my father didn't even get mad. (*Later in life I realized it was because he needed cigarettes, something to eat and someone to go to the store for him.*) He handed me three dollars. He said that was all he had, and out of that money I had to buy him two packs of cigarettes. I grabbed the money and got ready to run to the milk store, which was about a mile or so away. I put *two* flannel shirts on, and ran out the door, and into the snow storm.

A NICKEL IN MY SHOE

It was so cold, snowy and windy. There was about ten inches or more of snow already on the ground. I was freezing, but more than that I was starving. I made it to the store in about twenty minute's time. The cigarettes I bought came to $.70. I had enough money left to buy a box of chocolate donuts and a quart of milk. I sat outside of the store and choked down half the box of donuts, and guzzled half of the quart of milk. I forgot all about being cold for that few minutes. I saved the remaining donuts and milk for my father. I was hoping he didn't want any so I'd have something to eat later on. I ran all the way home. My father was equally as hungry as I was and ate the rest of the donuts.

It was so nice to go to bed with a full stomach. The burning feeling was gone, which made it much easier to fall asleep. I longed for *real* food though-maybe a hamburger, some mashed potatoes and corn. Just thinking about it made my mouth water. I was thankful just to have eaten *some* food. I don't think I could've survived another day without any.

I woke up shivering in the middle of the night. I was so cold, nauseated, and my throat hurt so badly. It felt as it was on fire and closing up. I had two large lumps in my neck, which made it very difficult to swallow, and my head was pounding. I wanted to get off of the couch to wake my father, but couldn't muster the energy. I simply lay there, and drifted in and out of sleep until my father walked in to the living room the following day.

It had to have been about noontime. He told me to get up so that he could sit there to watch TV. I told him I couldn't get up, that I was sick with a sore throat. I asked him to please get more blankets for me because I was freezing, and a pail to vomit in because I didn't think I could make it to the bathroom. He

82

appeared aggravated. I could tell that he was trying hard to control his temper. He said there were no more blankets in the house, and he threw a cooking pot at me to throw up in. He was fuming at the fact that he had to sit on the floor to watch television.

I was *extremely* thirsty. I was hungry as well, but couldn't eat even if there was food in the cupboards. My throat was too inflamed. I could barely swallow, and began to drool. My throat was getting worse, and my fever was getting so high that I started hallucinating. One of my hallucinations was that of hairpins chasing me.

My throat hurt so terribly that by the end of the day I began to cry. I started to plead with my father to please take me to a doctor, and to get me some water, or go to the store to buy juice. I begged him for some medicine to take the pain away as well.

My father became enraged. He began to swear and yell at me. "What the fuck, why did you go and get sick? I have no fuckin' money for a fuckin' doctor."

I saw his tongue come out of his mouth, and at that moment I knew I was going to get a beating. He proceeded to rip me off of the couch by my left arm, and he started to *pound* on me. I didn't have the strength to plead with him. It hurt too much to talk. He continued to swear and yell at me while holding me off the floor by my arm, at the same time he was hitting me with his other hand. I felt as if I was going to die, or at the very least my arm would break. He was so furious that I truly thought he was going to beat me to death. He flung me on to the couch and stormed out the front door.

I layed on that couch for what felt like days. I was hoping the entire time that someone would come and rescue me.

A NICKEL IN MY SHOE

I was starving, freezing, thirsty and delirious from having a high fever. I was nauseated as well, but there wasn't anything in my stomach to get rid of, therefore I only dry heaved, which, in turn, made my throat spasm, and my head hurt more.

I became so desperate that I called my mother, but her phone was disconnected. She had moved and never notified my father or me. I then called the kids that I used to hang out with in Orland Beach and asked to speak with their mother. I was trying to explain to her how sick I was, and that my father had been gone for days. She could hardly understand what I was saying because my throat was just about swollen shut. She asked what my address was so that she could send her husband to pick me up.

CHAPTER SEVENTEEN

SAVED

While waiting for Mr. Connor to arrive, I was laying on the couch. I kept floating in and out of consciousness, hallucinating that I was drinking all kinds of wonderful iced juices and water, but every time I went to take a sip I would wake up.

Then I heard a knock at the door. It was Mr. Connor- a short, stocky man with slicked back hair. He spoke with a southern drawl. I don't think I was ever as glad to see someone in my life, as I was to see him. He took one look at me and said, "Oh my God girl, what happened to you?!" I couldn't answer. He wrapped me up in a blanket and carried me to his car. I asked him to blast the heat. I felt so relieved. It was so nice and warm in his car that I slept all the way to their house. Mr. Connor carried me in to the house and placed me on a recliner chair in the living room. When Mrs. Connor took my temperature, it was 105.0. She then barked an order for someone to get me a (crushed) aspirin and juice. What little I managed to swallow came right back up.

Mr. and Mrs. Connor immediately began to try to track down my parents. My father was nowhere to be found, and somehow they discovered where my mother was living, and her phone number. Mrs. Connor called my mother repeatedly for hours. She never answered the phone. The next morning Mrs. Connor called the state and informed them of the situation. The assigned social worker went to my mothers' house. While there, my mother informed her that she didn't want me any more and was willing to give up her parental rights and sign me over to the state. The social worker had my mother fill out the necessary paper work, and presented it to a judge. I became a ward of the state that day. Mr. and Mrs. Conner told the social worker that they were willing to be my temporary foster parents, and stressed that it had to be done quickly because I needed immediate medical attention. They expedited the process and Mr. Connor took me to the hospital that evening.

It's not surprising that Mr. and Mrs. Connor helped me the way they did. They always opened their door to poor souls like me. There wasn't a time that I could remember that they didn't have someone living with them, whether it was a wayward family member or a stranger down on their luck. You might think these people were very kind and caring but their acts of kindness always came with a price. If a person living there collected unemployment or disability checks-they took them. If they had no money-they cleaned and served Mrs. Connor as if she was royalty. Even putting her on a bed pan if she didn't feel like getting up to use the bathroom-which was quite often. When they took *me* in, I wanted so much to believe that someone on this earth loved me and cared about me. The truth was, what they saw in me was a state pay check- they were protecting their investment. No matter what the reason was-they saved my life.

I did get the medical care that I needed. If it wasn't for the Connor's, my infection may have gone systemic and I surely would have died. I don't understand, till this day, why my parents didn't get charged with child abuse and neglect. I didn't understand how they got away with this atrocity. I couldn't comprehend why nobody cared-even the people that were *paid* to care-didn't.

The Connor's were appalled by the fact that I didn't own a coat. Mrs. Connor was a tall woman with long brown hair. I could see where she probably was once a very attractive woman. But, she had incredibly vulgar language. The "F" word was included at least once in every sentence. She had a harsh whisky voice, and yelled when she spoke. She was a very domineering woman. People, including her own husband, and certainly her children were afraid of her. They all went to great lengths to appease her. I was so happy that she liked me. No one ever wanted to be on *her* bad side.

Mrs. Connor decided that she would take me clothes shopping. I felt special because not even her *own* children received brand new clothes-ever, at least not until today.

We all piled in the car; the six kids, me and Mr. and Mrs. Connor *(and Mrs. Connors wheelchair.)* We went to a bargain-clothing store. Mrs. Connor told me to pick out a coat, three pairs of pants and three shirts. The only stipulation is that they had to be chosen from the sales racks. All of the children were so happy for me. One might think they'd be envious or resentful, but they weren't. I told Mrs. Connor that I felt uncomfortable because I was the only one getting any new clothing. She thought about it for a few minutes then let each child pick out one outfit and a pair of sneakers. They were ecstatic. These were their first new clothes ever. This was the first time that I've ever witnessed her being nice to her children—and it was the last.

A few months had passed. I was attending a new junior high school with the Connor kids. None of us went to school very often. We were forced to stay home and clean the house-all day and all night long. The Connor children continued to endure the punishments given to them by their parents, mostly their mother. However, she never was physically abusive to me.

As time went by, I began to get very home sick. I missed Karen immensely. I didn't miss the beatings from my mother, but I sure did miss the food, clean clothes and my comfortable bed—none of which my father or the Connor's provided for me.

My father visited me on occasion, but his stopovers were brief, and most likely out of guilt. Once in a while, I snuck and called my mother. She didn't return any of my calls until one day in late fall. She called to tell me she was pregnant and getting married. She was marrying the man that accompanied her to the house the night when my sister and I were molested.

I became very excited at the thought of having a new baby brother or sister. I loved babies so very much. When I was a little girl, I would beg my mother to have a baby just for me.

I was only about 5 or 6-years-old when I informed my mother that Shawn and I wanted a baby of our own, and asked her how we could get one. She said, "Well, *you* lay on one side of the bed, and *Shawn* is to lie on the other side of the bed, then you both wish to God for a baby at the same time. I immediately ran to Shawn's house at the top of the hill, and dragged him home with me. I told him what my mother had said. I forced him to lie on one side of the bed, and I laid on the other. I gave him strict instructions on what we were to do next.

"O.K," I said. "I'm going to count to three and, at the same time, we are to wish for a baby. Ready…1…2…3…wish! I closed my eyes tight and thought really hard. "Oh please God, please give Shawn and me a baby."

SAVED

I opened my eyes. I asked Shawn if he wished really hard. He said he did. I jumped off of the bed and ran to the bedroom door and opened it. There was no baby waiting there for me outside of the door. I was very disappointed. I told Shawn that he must not have wished hard enough. I got back on my side of the bed and told him to wish again, but this time he has to wish harder. We did this about five more times, to no avail. My mother was in the kitchen listening to us, I could hear her giggling. Feeling disappointed and frustrated, I went running to her and told her that God didn't leave a baby for us yet. She was trying to hold back her laughter, and told me maybe God thought we were too young, and to wait till we were married. I told her that she was going to have to have a baby for me. She broke into hysterical laughter.

The news of her pregnancy only made my desire to live with my mother that much stronger. I asked her if I could, but, she said no. When asked why, she would avoid the question and make up a lame excuse to end our conversation.

I felt disappointed, lonely and lost every time we ended our phone call because I knew I wouldn't be able to speak with her again for a long while.

Thanksgiving had come and gone. I waited by the phone all day long and neither my mother nor father called to wish me a happy holiday. That night I went to bed and cried myself to sleep.

Christmas was just around the corner. This will be my first Christmas without my mother or my sister. It felt strange not to belong to a *real* family.

I began to call the bar where my father spent most of his time. They always had the same answer for me—he wasn't there. Finally, one day he came to the phone. I told him how much I missed him and begged to spend Christmas with him and Leigha. He finally agreed. He told me he would pick me up the morning of the 24th. I felt both relieved and afraid simultaneously; relieved to spend Christmas with a family member, and afraid because of my father's terrible temper.

CHAPTER EIGHTEEN

HORROR NEXT DOOR

The morning of the 24th was finally here. I woke up early, took a bath and sat on the front steps for hours. I tried to avoid Mrs. Connor because she was angry with me for wanting to go with my father. She asked me, "Why do you want to go and visit that lousy fuck anyway?" Although her words cut me like a knife, I tried explaining to her that it wasn't personal, and that I appreciated all that she has done for me, but it was important that I see my father. Again, she asked me why. I told her I didn't know why. I couldn't put the reason into words. I told her that I had a strong need, and didn't understand it myself. I asked her not to be angry with me because that made me feel afraid. She just turned her head and looked the other way.

I was relieved to see my fathers' car coming down the street. I was starting to feel disappointed because it was getting dark outside, and I was beginning to think he was going to stand me up, as he had done so many times before.

I was so happy to be spending Christmas with him. I told him how much I've been missing him. He reciprocated. I wanted to believe that he missed me to, but there was insincerity in his voice.

A NICKEL IN MY SHOE

When we arrived at the house I was shocked to see both Leigha and Mary there. My father never mentioned that Mary would be spending Christmas with us. It had been a long time since we've seen each other. She felt like a stranger to me. I didn't know what to say or do. It was an awkward moment. She was her usual miserable self. I decided that I was going to stay out of her way the best that I could without offending her.

Leigha had put up the Christmas tree. It had lights and a few decorations on it, but there were no presents under the tree. It was nothing compared to the way my mother decorated *her* tree. There were hundreds of lights, tinsel, bells, balls and she even sprayed fake snow on it, not to mention the tons of presents that she placed under it.

There were *no* presents under my father and Leighas' tree. It didn't feel like Christmas in that house. It was cold and uninviting. Leigha and my father weren't getting along either, and I started getting nervous.

I was hungry, but I was afraid to say so, or to ask for anything to eat. It was all too fresh in my mind what happened to me the last time I asked my father for something. There was old cheese and crackers on the table from earlier in the day, so I helped myself to what was left and hoped it didn't make me sick.

Mary and I could sense that Leigha and my father were not getting along so we decided to go to bed. My father told us to sleep in his bed that night. I didn't mind going to bed a little bit early because it gave my father time to place all our presents under the tree.

Mary and I laid there in silence. After a while she began to speak "Dad is a bum," she said. "Are you really stupid enough to think that he got us anything for Christmas?" "Of course he got us Christmas presents," I responded. "How could he not? It's Christmas time. No kid goes without presents." "You really are a retard," she said. "You really are an idiot." I didn't know what to say. I was afraid to say anything at all.

We were lying there when we heard Leigha and my father start to argue. The master bedroom was quite far from the living room, so we couldn't make out exactly what they were saying. The tones of their voices, however, were harsh.

The next thing we heard was the door to Leighas' sons' bedroom slam shut. They were going to sleep in *his* room because he was spending the night with his father.

The yelling became louder. My father was calling Leigha all of the vulgar names he used to call my mother. Next I heard what sounded as if my father slammed her on to the bed. Leigha began to cry and beg him, "No Bobby, I don't want to turn over…please don't…that hurts…you're hurting me… get off of me." Then I hear low growls and grunts with muffled screams at times. I was bewildered about the sounds I was hearing. It scared me so badly that I crawled under the blankets to hide. I asked Mary what she thought was going on in there.

"He's raping her," she said, nonchalantly. "He does that a lot, and I'm sick of having to listen to it all the time."

My stomach felt so sick I thought I was going to vomit, but I didn't dare get out of bed! I laid there awake for the rest of the night, listening to the brutal horror that was taking place in the bedroom next door. I was too afraid to go to sleep.

I waited for the sun to come up before even thinking about getting out of bed. I nudged Mary so she would wake up. I was too scared to get out of bed alone. I asked her to come out in to the living room with me to see all the presents. She did.

I think she was hoping she would be wrong, and there would be presents waiting for us.

"I told you so you dumb fuck!" she said in a disgusted tone of voice.

The disappointment I felt for both my sister and myself was monumental. It was devastating not to receive toys or (much needed) clothes for Christmas.

Mary was furious as well as fed up with my father's irresponsibility. She went marching in to his room to wake him up.

"Get up, it's Christmas," she said. "You have kids you know."

He came running out of the bedroom. Before he could even respond to Mary's words, she said in a disgusted, demonic tone, "Since you didn't buy us anything for Christmas the *least* you can do is make us breakfast."

Well, my father went ballistic. He lunged at her, hitting her as he screamed, "Who the fuck are *you* to be telling *me* to make you breakfast. You can fuckin' starve to death for all I care, you little fuckin' no good bitch!"

He stormed off into the bedroom, got dressed and left the house." My sister didn't flinch. She bravely stood there and took the beating he doled out. I, on the other hand, hid in the corner and cowered. I thought for certain he was going to beat me next. When my father became that angry he lost all self-control, he would hit *any* person or object that got in his way.

Leigha emerged from the bedroom after my father stormed out of the house. Her cheek was bruised, as well as having bruises on her arms in the shape of fingers. I was stunned by her appearance. I ran to her and hugged her. I told her I was

94

sorry for what he did to her. She hugged me back. She said she was sorry too.

Leigha told Mary that she had to find another place to live. She also said that she was leaving my father, and then drove me back to the Connor's house.

CHAPTER NINETEEN

A NEW BABY BROTHER TO LOVE

Life continued as usual until I received a phone call one cold day in January of 1975. It was one of the very few days that I actually attended school. I was in Art class and the teacher handed me the classroom phone. It was Mary telling me that my mother had a baby boy that morning. She named him Guy David, and that he weighed five pounds. I felt so excited and proud to have a new baby brother. However, I soon began to feel sadness because I didn't know if I was ever going to be allowed to see him.

My mother spent a week in the hospital. She called me the week after that to ask if I wanted to come over to see the new baby. I felt like jumping for joy, but all I could muster was a meek "yes." I had to hide my happiness because I was afraid if I showed how excited I really was, my mother would mistake that for bad behavior and not allow me to see my new brother.

My mother said that she would pick me up on Saturday morning. I could hardly stand the excitement I felt that week. I thought I was going to jump out of my skin.

Saturday was here. I was nervous because I hadn't seen my mother or Karen in what felt like forever. In all actuality it was about eight months. Mrs. Connor didn't understand how I could possibly want to see my mother after she had abandoned me. She displayed her disapproval by calling my mother all kinds of bad names- including the "C" word and by giving me the silent treatment all the way up until the minute my mother arrived to pick me up. Mrs. Connor was trying to make me feel guilty. It worked, but, the excitement of having a new baby brother, coupled with seeing my mother and sister over powered my feelings of guilt. I was also quite curious about, and anxious to formerly meet my new stepfather.

When my mother beeped the horn I immediately ran out and jumped in her car. I was disappointed to see that she came to pick me up alone. I was hoping that my sister would be there too, but she wasn't. My mother was acting strange, as if she had a wall up between us. She didn't say anything to me such as hello, or I miss you. Nothing. She was polite enough though, and answered my numerous questions. However, she offered no conversation on her own. When she spoke she had no anima-tion in her voice, it was completely monotone. She acted as if she was being coerced in to doing something that she didn't want to do. I didn't have the guts to ask her the one question that I really wanted to ask her- If I could come back home. I was too afraid of the answer. I was fearful of being rejected again. I could feel the tension between us in the air, but I was too happy and excited to care.

We finally made it to her house. On the way in to the com-plex I noticed a built in swimming pool and tennis courts. I thought my new stepfather must be rich because only rich people could afford such luxuries. The name of the apartment complex was Fairfax Village. The apartments were built side-by-side, town house style and each apartment had three levels.

A NEW BABY BROTHER TO LOVE

I walked in to the foyer landing and noticed the distinctive layout. To my left were stairs leading up to the two bedrooms, and the other set of stairs lead down to the kitchen, dining area and bathroom. The third set of stairs lead down into the living room area. The apartment was small, yet unique, and had a cozy feel to it.

Karen came running down stairs to greet me. We both jumped at each other to hug and almost fell down the flight of stairs. We were both crying, and telling each other how much we missed each other. My mother stood there with her arms folded and had a blank look on her face. I would have given anything to know what she was thinking at that very moment.

Karen had matured immensely in the eight months since I've seen her. She was incredibly pretty. Her hair grew long and she was taller then me. She had shed her little girl appearance and was becoming a young lady.

I immediately asked them where the baby was. Karen lead me up the stairs and in to the master bedroom, where the crib was. My mother didn't follow us. I peaked in and saw a tiny little baby. His arms and legs were flailing about. He had dark hair and bright blue eyes. I have never seen a color like that in my entire life. It looked as if someone had applied black eyeliner around both of his eyes; in turn making the blue color of his eyes appear deeper and more intense. (*My brother would be known by people for the rest of his life as "Guy with the eyes"*).

I picked him up, kissed and cuddled him. I felt overjoyed. I finally had the baby that I always dreamed of. My Nana taught me to make a wish to God when holding a baby for the first time. As I cuddled little Guy, I prayed to God and wished that he would have a happy life.

A NICKEL IN MY SHOE

I asked Karen where his diapers were because I wanted to change him. He didn't need changing, but I wanted to anyway. After changing him I asked if I could feed him. It wasn't time for him to eat my mother said, but she gave me a bottle with two ounces of formula in it anyway. I rocked him as he ate. I fell immediately in love with my baby brother, and knew I didn't want to leave him.

When my new stepfather came home, my mother formerly introduced us. His name was Fred. He was a short, well-proportioned man with blonde hair and piercing blue eyes.

"It's nice to finally meet you," Fred said with an upbeat voice. He began to say funny things and joke around with Karen. Hearing them interact made me feel relieved. I had been so afraid that he was being cruel to her. He gave me the impression of being genuinely nice. I liked him.

Later in the afternoon my mother told me it was time for her to take me *home*. I felt my heart drop. I didn't want to leave. I felt as if I *was* home.

As time went on I became even more home sick. Not so much for my mother, but for my baby brother and Karen. I missed the good food and comfortable bed as well. I began to call my mother continuously to tell her I was sorry, and ask her if I could please come home. Finally, one day, she returned my phone call and said yes. I was ecstatic, however, the Connor's were not.

It was now April of 1975- I was thirteen-years-old. Once again, after moving in with my mother, I was enrolled in yet another school. I didn't mind though because I was with my family. I loved being with Karen again, however, she was different. She was oddly quiet. This made me somewhat uneasy. I thought maybe she was angry with me for leaving her.

A NEW BABY BROTHER TO LOVE

My brother was three-months-old and I thoroughly enjoyed taking care of him. I hardly let anyone else hold him, change him or feed him. I even awoke in the middle of the night to help care for him. I could sense that this irritated my mother but she never said anything. What I didn't enjoy was the enormous amount of chores that I had to do-such as *all* the cleaning, and everyone's laundry. I had to wash the clothes at the complex laundry room-but I was not allowed to dry them in a dryer. I had to carry them back, wet, and hang them on the clothesline in our back yard. This was very hard work. I had to hang the pants with the pants, shirts with shirts, towels with towels, all according to size and color. If one piece of clothing was out of place, my mother would tear them all off the clothes line and make me start over. Sometimes it took me all day to hang one basket of laundry on the clothesline.

It wasn't fair. Karen could go out and play with her friends, but I couldn't. Taking care of the baby and doing all the housework, along with my school responsibilities, consumed my life. My mother made sure that I had no time for fun.

The weather was getting warmer. It was nice to see the sunshine, hear the birds sing and smell the new spring flowers.

I asked my mother if I could take Guy for a walk to the store because I needed some personal items, she said yes. I dressed him in his cutest outfit, covered him with a blanket and strapped him in his stroller. It was gorgeous outside. The wind was chilly, but the sun felt warm. I felt so proud and grown-up to be taking my baby brother for a walk. It was the only time in my life that I felt content. The birth of Guy was the best thing that ever happened to me. I loved both him and Karen more than life itself.

A NICKEL IN MY SHOE

While shopping, people would stop me to say how beautiful Guy was, and how they have never seen eyes that blue before. They asked me if he was mine. I wanted to say yes, but I didn't. I told them I was only thirteen and Guy was my brother.

On the way home from the store, I decided that the weather was too nice to go straight home, and thought the fresh air would be healthy for my brother, so I decided to sit on the wooden rails that separated the busy main road, from the apartment complex entrance-there was a side walk in-between.

Guy had fallen asleep, and I was sitting on the rail soaking up the sun when a blue car pulled up on the side of me as if it was going to enter the complex. The man driving wore an officer's uniform. He was handsome, with light brown wavy hair, and appeared to be fairly young-maybe in his mid 20's, early 30's.

He stopped, flashed a badge and asked me, "Weren't you just at the station?" I asked him to repeat himself and he did. I told him that he must be mistaken, that I was out taking my brother for a walk, and that he had the wrong person. He said, "I am not mistaken, you were just arrested. You were just at the police station. NOW GET IN THE CAR!"

I became extremely frightened, and began to shake. I wasn't as afraid for myself as I was for my brother's safety. I grabbed the baby carriage and ran as fast as I could. I had to run by his car to make it up the driveway to my apartment. He began to chase me all the while yelling for me to get into his car. I made it to my front steps and he pulled a u-turn and sped off, out of the apartment complex. I ran in to tell my mother, and she called the police. They arrived shortly thereafter to take a report. I wasn't one to defy authority. I may have obeyed him out of trust and respect, and entered his car if I didn't have my brother with me that day.

It was disheartening because the very people in life who were supposed to be my protectors ended up hurting me and deceiving me the most. I felt as if all hope was gone because now I couldn't even depend on the police to keep me safe. I was afraid of them too.

CHAPTER TWENTY

THE BEATING OF MY LIFE

Summer was finally here and school was ending-but what I was most excited about was that the complex pool would be opening for the summer season. I begged my mother to let me go to the pool on opening day. To my surprise, she said I could, and reminded me that I had to baby-sit that evening for Kathy -a lady that lived near the Conner's. I told her that I didn't forget.

I ran to get my bathing suit on, grabbed a towel and headed off to the pool. When I stuck my toe in the water- it felt ice cold. I decided not to go swimming and thought I would just sun bathe instead. I found a sunny spot on the pool deck, set my lounge chair up, applied my baby oil, turned my radio on and got comfortable.

I was getting a little bored. I was the only young person there, and thought about going home, but decided not too because I knew my mother would only make me do house work. The sun felt so good on my face. It relaxed me so much that I soon fell asleep.

Sometime later on in the day, the lifeguard woke me up saying, "Hey there, you're getting awfully red. You'd better turn over or cover up." I thanked her and rolled over onto my stomach, but the entire front of me stung to high heaven. I decided it was time to go home- whether I wanted to or not.

After arriving home, I began to get ready to go babysitting. While in the shower, I couldn't stand the drops of water hitting my skin. Every drop felt like a slap and even though the water was on the cool setting it still felt hot. My body seemed redder after taking a shower then it was before I got into the shower. As the evening wore on my sunburn became more red and painful and my skin was becoming tighter.

Kathy, the lady I was babysitting for, came to pick me up at 7:00 p.m. I was finding it difficult to walk because I couldn't straighten out my knees. It was as if the skin on my legs had no elasticity. Kathy was concerned and asked if I was all right. "Maybe you should stay home," she said. But I told her I'd be fine.

By the time we arrived at her house I was practically in tears. The entire front of my body was burning, especially my legs, and I could barely walk. Kathy was a nurse and thought I needed to be seen at the hospital. She called my mother to receive permission to take me. Kathy gave up her night on the town with her friends to take me to the emergency room.

When we got there I could barely walk. I was in dire pain. After Kathy checked me in, the emergency room nurse wheeled me back to a room and helped me to get on the examination table. She proceeded to fill a basin with cool water and gently placed wet cloths on my legs. But it felt as if she was *slapping* them on my legs. There are no words to describe that type of pain, the best one I can think of is excruciating. The doctor came in to examine me and said I had second-degree sunburn. He suggested that I place cool cloths on my legs for the next few days, and gave Kathy a prescription for pain pills. After picking up the pain medication Kathy took me back to her house, by which time my legs started to blister and I couldn't walk. She carried me into the house and placed me on a couch by the front window in the den. She gave me a pain pill but it didn't work. I couldn't sleep a wink and I cried most of the night because the pain was so horrendous.

Kathy came in the next morning and asked if she could get me anything. I asked her for *two* pain pills this time, a cigarette and a glass of juice. I took my pills and lit my cigarette. I was laying there on the couch trying to find a comfortable position when my mother and Fred walked up the porch steps. They were looking through the window at me while I was smoking. I turned around and when I saw them I felt the blood rush from my face. I began to tremble with fear.

My mother has caught me smoking many times before. She would scream in my face how I better not smoke again and to teach me a lesson, she made me eat cigarettes until I vomited. That is what I thought I was in for this time as well. I was wrong.

She came crashing through the front door. She ran over to the couch I was laying on. She began yelling, "How dare you-you stupid little bitch. This is what you do when I let you out of my sight?" She continued to call me names and scream obscenities at me. She grabbed me by my hair and yanked me off the couch. I fell to the floor because I couldn't walk, which I was trying to tell her through my screams of pain. She dragged me over to another couch that was in the family room and threw me on to it. I was screaming for Kathy, whom I think was hiding in the kitchen. She finally came running out into the family room. She was begging my mother not to hurt me anymore and was trying to place the blame on herself in order to save me- Kathy was *desperately* trying to reason with her. I couldn't hear what my mother was saying to her because I was screaming from the pain, but I think it had something to do with Kathy allowing me to smoke. Fred and my mother were standing there in front of me when she told him to take his (leather) belt off. He said, "No Paige, you can't mean that." Kathy continued begging her not to hurt me. She screamed at him to take it off or she would do it for him. I couldn't believe my ears. I couldn't fathom what she was about to do to me. I wanted to die right then and there or at the very least pass out. I knew I couldn't even run away from the beating, I was stuck on that couch unable to escape. I started screaming for someone to please stop her. No one did. They just looked on in horror and disbelief-I think Kathy was in shock.

She began to whip me with the belt- aiming specifically for my legs. I was screaming and trying to protect my legs- then she would whip my arms and hands, which were also burnt. She wouldn't stop. I threw myself onto the floor and tried to crawl away. She continued to follow me- whipping me with the belt on my back until she had me backed in to a corner against the wall. My head felt numb- I felt dizzier and weaker with every 'whip' of the belt. Kathy ran for the phone but my mother told her that if she called the police she (my mother) would press charges against her. I don't know what sort of charges, but that is what my mother threatened. Kathy backed down. She placed her hands over her nose and mouth and cried. I felt so helpless and alone at that moment.

Fred stood in the middle of the room and didn't utter a word for the entire time I was getting whipped. I got the impression that he started to *enjoy* the horror show that my mother was putting on for everyone. He could have stopped my mother if he really wanted to, but he didn't. He just stood there watching in complete silence.

My mother *finally* stopped whipping me. My legs would tighten up then relax; it's as if they would spasm. I had white strap marks all over my sun burnt body- my skin had turned white where ever the strap had landed - in a criss-cross type pattern. My mother grabbed me by my hair and told me to get up and walk. I told her through sobs that I couldn't. She said if I didn't that she would drag me down the (wooden) porch steps, across the pavement and into the car. I tried to get on my feet but my legs wouldn't straighten out, they kept buckling and I would fall down. She accused me of faking- and was yelling that it wasn't as bad as I was making it out to be. I tried three or four times until she lost her patience. She told me I was pathetic, and then she grabbed me by my hair and dragged me down the steps and threw me in to the car. I tried my best to keep from scraping my legs on the ground, but I didn't do a very good job of it.

I couldn't help but hold my breath and sob. What I really wanted to do was scream and cry- but I didn't dare. She told me that I got what I deserved, and to shut up. When we arrived home, she dragged me out of the car, by my arm this time. She brought me in the house and pulled me downstairs to the living room couch and threw me on it. She said watch this; she walked into the bathroom and proceeded to flush my pain medication down the toilet. My mother told me I could rot to death on the couch for all she cared.

I couldn't walk for three days, and in that time the most I could do was crawl to the toilet. I wasn't allowed to eat or drink until I could walk to get food on my own. My legs started to blister in the shape of belt marks. She warned me if my legs got infected that she wasn't taking me to the doctor and that I could crawl there myself. She also ordered Karen and Fred not to speak to me or get me anything to eat or drink, and if they did they would be in major trouble. She said I better get off the couch soon because the laundry was piling up and that was my responsibility. *Everything* was my responsibility.

After the sunburn incident, my mother became even crueler. I was enslaved in that house for months; taking care of my baby brother, doing all the laundry, and cleaning the house from top to bottom. I was *never* allowed to leave, except to wash the laundry at the complex launder mat. I wasn't even allowed to take Guy for walks anymore. My sister had friends and could go out to play but I wasn't allowed to have any friends. I started to become extremely miserable and soon the arguing began.

I was hanging out the laundry when my mother came crashing through the back door. She came charging at me and began to slap me while hollering that I wasn't "doing it right." "How many fuckin' times do I have to tell you how to hang laundry on a god damn clothes line?" She growled through gritted teeth. She began to tear the wet laundry off of the clothesline, yelling all the while how incompetent I was. She said "now, start over, and you better get it right, or I'll rip'em off the line again and again, until you get it right!"

I said, "No," and told her that I refuse to be her slave any longer. She picked up her hand and slapped me across the face as hard as she could. I went flying backwards and hit my head on the ground. Everything started to go dark at that point; I was fighting to stay awake-to not pass out. My head was spinning and I couldn't see straight. I got up off the ground and told her I hated her, and that I was leaving.

THE BEATING OF MY LIFE

I left the house, with only the clothes on my back, and ran to the store where they had a pay phone. I was nervous that my father wouldn't come to the phone when I called the bar room. I called the operator to place a collect phone call; just when the bar tender said he wouldn't accept the call, I said, very quickly, that I had no where to go and needed desperately to talk to my father. The man accepted the call. He told me my father really wasn't there, but he would give him the message when he arrived. I gave him the location of the store and waited for what seemed like hours. I was so afraid my father wouldn't come to rescue me. I waited until well after dark. He never showed up.

CHAPTER TWENTY-ONE

THE INSTITUTION

My mother pulled up along side of me in her car. She angrily told me that my father called her to say he wasn't going to pick me up. She ordered me to get into the car. I didn't have any other choice, so I obeyed her command. She said she was taking me to Nana's house to live. I felt happy and relieved. I loved Nana with all of my heart and soul. We didn't say a word to each other for the entire ride to Nana's apartment. When we arrived, I got out of the car and slammed the door shut. I didn't look back to see if my mother was following behind me or not. I didn't care either way. I got on the elevator alone.

By this time Nana lived in a high rise apartment building on the 12th floor. It was much nicer than her last apartment. She used to complain about the lady that lived above her. She was a prostitute and brought bed bugs home- which spread to all three apartments in the building. She also said that the woman would give her three small children medicine everyday in order to make them sleep so that she could *work*.

Nana's new apartment was small but bright, new and clean. It had only one bedroom so I had to sleep on the couch. When I walked in she didn't act happy to see me like she usually did.

She actually looked angry. I thought she was mad at me, but looking back, I think she was actually mad (and disappointed) at my mother.

She did the best she could for being an elderly woman trying to care for a young girl of thirteen. Since it was summer and she didn't know what to do with me during the week, she signed me up to attend the YMCA. It was about a mile away from the high rise. I was afraid because I had to walk there alone and it was one of the most crime-ridden neighborhoods in the entire state. I sucked it up and did as I was told. I just kept telling myself to be brave.

I felt as if I didn't belong there. The kids were tough, and weren't afraid of anything or anyone. I on the other hand was not tough, and was afraid of everything and everyone. All I did at the Y was hang out by the juke box all day long and play the same songs over and over again; "Wild Horses" and "Angie" both by the Rolling Stones.

Nana wasn't very nice to me anymore. She appeared worried, as if her mind was preoccupied. She never smiled and didn't speak to me very much. There was tension in the air, and I didn't know why. She wasn't her usual kind and happy self. She no longer took me on the bus to the city, like she used to every now and again. I loved it when she took me downtown to Woolworth's. They had an eatery that sold banana splits. There were balloons hanging off the ceiling; enclosed in each one was a special price for the banana splits. I would pick a balloon and pop it. Once I popped a balloon, and the price was one cent. She was thrilled that she only had to pay a penny for my banana split. It made me happy too, because I loved to please her.

Nana continued her nightly drinking binges. She would rant and rave for hours on end about how she didn't want to do what my mother was forcing her to do. I didn't understand what she was talking about. I begged her to tell me but she wouldn't. All I knew is that she wasn't acting normal, and that something wasn't quite right; I could sense it- on one hand I wanted desperately to know, but on the other hand, I was afraid to find out what my mother was forcing her to do.

Finally it was Monday- and I was glad. Nana hardly spoke to me for the entire weekend. It was unbearable. I couldn't tell if she was mad or sad. I was happy, for once, to be going to the YMCA; it would get me away from the awful tension that filled the apartment.

I started to get ready for the day. I ran my bath water and laid out my clothes. After I was dressed, Nana said to me "Susan, you're not going to the YMCA today. Someone is coming to pick you up."

"Who?" I asked- surprised. She didn't answer. Then, she sat in her chair and stared straight ahead. She said only two more words to me and they were "I'm sorry." I became terrified.

Suddenly, the doorbell rang. Nana hesitated before opening the door. A police officer and a woman dressed in a business suit walked in, and introduced themselves to my grandmother. I asked them what was happening, and if I was in trouble. They didn't answer me. The only thing they said to me was that I had to go with them, and that they couldn't tell me where they were taking me. I wrapped my arms around Nana and clung to her as tight as I could. I was begging and pleading with her not to let them take me away. I told her I wanted to stay there with her forever, but she remained cold and distant. She pried my arms from around her waist, while the officer peeled me off of her. The woman in the business suit took hold of one arm, and the police officer took hold of my other arm, and led me away;

I screamed and cried for Nana to save me the entire way to the car. It killed me inside to think the one person on the face of the earth that I believed loved me- didn't. I was crushed.

I cried and sobbed for the entire ride. "Where are you taking me?" I continued to ask them both over and over again between sobs. "What did I do wrong?"

They never uttered one word in response. I was so scared. I thought I was going to prison, and I didn't understand what I did wrong.

We pulled up to the creepiest building that I have ever seen in my life. *This can't be happening, this can't be real,* I thought to myself. It looked like a dreary, old and worn out castle. I assumed it was a jail.

The structure was built out of gray cement that they never washed or painted and it had to have been at least two hundred years old. It had black streaks running down the entire front of it. Thick, rusty iron bars covered all the windows. There were several of these structures lined up in a row. There were workers dressed in white uniforms as well as people in plain, dull clothes walking on the grounds and between the buildings. They didn't look like people. They looked more like zombies. They moved slowly, and their faces were dull and expressionless.

They took me out of the car and physically escorted me up the main steps, down three long corridors, and into a musty smelling office.

The interior of the building was as dark and dreary as the exterior was. The hallways smelled horrible like decaying meat masked by cheap institutional cleaning solvent. I was so frightened and bewildered. I wondered what I did so wrong that I had to go to jail. But I finally stopped asking. I didn't want to irritate them anymore than I already have. I was on *their* territory now and I knew they could do anything they wanted to me. Nobody would stop them. Nobody would save me.

A woman made me go in to a back room and told me to take off all my clothes. She looked and sounded more like a male than she did a female. The only way I could tell she was a woman was because she had enormous boobs. I was sure that they rested on her knees when she sat down.

I told her I couldn't get undressed in front of her because I was too embarrassed. I begged for her to *please* call my father to come and take me home, but she paid no attention to my pleas.

I continued to beg while I was, ever so slowly, taking my clothes off. Finally, she spoke to me.

"Sorry to be the bearer of bad news," she said. "But you *are* home honey, and unless you're stupid, you should have figured out by now that *nobody* wants you! Now shut up and take off your fuckin' clothes or I'll rip'em off. I don't have time for your cry baby bullshit!"

Her words kept ringing in my ears; *nobody wants you.* Those words stung more than any beating I have ever received in my entire life. I continued to beg. "Please, please no, I'm embarrassed."

She started to walk toward me. I told her to stop- I would take them off.

I couldn't believe what was happening. I thought it was a bad dream, and that I would wake up any minute. What little self-esteem I had remaining was stripped away with each piece of clothing I removed. My dignity was replaced with shame. Any hope I had was replaced by despair.

I stood there naked, hoping I would die. Then she said, "Now bend over."

"WHAT?!" I screamed.

A NICKEL IN MY SHOE

"Gotta see if you're hiding anything. Now do it!"

Hide what and where? I thought to my self. I was absolutely mortified.

I have never felt as humiliated in my life as I did at that moment. I felt utterly violated, as if I got raped. I couldn't stop crying, and felt so hopeless. I realized at that moment how worthless and unwanted I was. I literally thought that I had died and went to hell. I never had much self esteem, however, what little I did have remaining was stripped away that day.

After my humiliating and degrading *cavity* search, the woman led me into to a large bathroom. There were ten showerheads in a row, and adjacent to them sat ten toilets. The room was totally open, with no partition between the stalls. She turned on the shower full force and told me to get under the water. I couldn't believe she was going to stand there and watch me! I wanted to turn invisible. She gave me a bar of soap, a squirt of shampoo and told me to wash myself starting with my hair. The shampoo smelled horrible, and the soap didn't smell any better. When I was finished, she gave me the ugliest looking outfit to wear. They were at least three sizes too big, stiff and they made me itchy.

She told me to follow her. She led me down a long corridor; I felt as if I went colorblind because everything was a dingy gray color, including the god-awful clothing she gave me to wear.

We passed a station where some workers were sitting. I could see them out of the corner of my eye, but I didn't dare look at them. I was too afraid. But mostly, I was ashamed. We stopped in front of a room. It was no bigger then a broom closet. It held a cot. That was it. The room had a very small window with rusty bars on it, and it stunk like vomit, feces, urine and bleach.

THE INSTITUTION

She told me that bedtime was at 8:00 p.m., and wake up was at 5:00 a.m., I was to immediately take a shower. She said if I didn't wake up on the first call and immediately report to the shower room that there would be a consequence. She said breakfast was at 6:00 a.m. sharp, and if I missed it I would starve until the following day. She went on to tell me that I needed to check the board by the workstation immediately following breakfast to see what chores I would be responsible for that day.

I asked her who was responsible for me being there and for how long I would be detained. She got right up in my face, nose to nose, backed me up against the wall and said "I'm only going to say this once, so listen up. If you ask me one more question pertaining to going *home*, I am going to knock all of your fuckin' teeth out, you got it? Now, get this through your thick head you stupid little bitch; YOU LIVE *HERE*. THIS IS YOUR *HOME AND I* AM YOUR *MOTHER* AND *FATHER* AND *I* DON'T LIKE YOU ALREADY! NOW SHUT THE FUCK UP! UNDERSTAND?" A meek yes ma'am was all I could muster. I promised myself that I would follow all the rules and *never* do anything wrong.

I was scared to death. All I could do every night is look out window through the rusty old bars and up to the heavens and ask God to please send someone to come and save me. I also told God that I was desperate to know what it was that I did wrong to get into prison, so that I could right my wrong, and never make that mistake again.

(This was an institution for wayward, as well as unwanted children)

I cried myself to sleep that night. When I woke up the next morning I was devastated to find out that this wasn't a bad dream and that I was actually living this nightmare. I found my way to the shower room, then to the cafeteria for breakfast then on to check the chore board. My chore that day was to sweep and mop the cafeteria and bathroom floors.

All the girls ignored me and this was just fine by me. There were about seven of them on my ward. I didn't look at any of them, but I could feel their eyes on *me*. We were allowed to watch one hour of television in the day room before lunch everyday. I was dreading this because I would be confronted with the girls on my ward all at once- in one small room. I didn't know if they were going to beat me up or maybe even kill me. I felt safer in the large cafeteria, where there were fifty or more people. I knew I had to act tough or they would eat me alive.

All seven of the girls were sprawled out on the three couches that were in the day room. I walked in and merely stood there. There was no place for me to sit and I was too nervous to ask someone to move over. I glanced at each of them for a second or two, they all were young but they looked hard, worn out, and old. I wondered if I looked like that too.

One of the girls asked if I wanted to sit next to her. I said yes, and thanks. I was so proud of myself that my response came out semi gruff and not meek. I felt it would've been detrimental to my physical health if they detected any kind of weakness or fear. She sat up straight and patted the cushion next to her and I sat down. I was so nervous that my hands began to sweat- I nonchalantly rubbed them on my pant legs to dry them off.

We all sat in awkward silence for a few minutes, when, finally, one of the girls asked me what I did wrong to get in there. I told her I didn't know. I threw out a question to the whole group, asking them what *they* did wrong to get in there.

THE INSTITUTION

I was surprised that most of them were trying to answer at the same time, and had smiles on their faces, as if they were *proud* to be there:

"I set my house on fire."

"I tried to stab my mother's boyfriend."

"My father raped me, and my mother said I was lying."

"I never go to school."

"I have sex with everyone."

"My mother said I was too hard to take care of."

The last girl didn't answer my question. I said, "Well, I haven't done *any* of that. My parents just don't want me I guess." They all laughed at me and called me a liar.

I went to my cell that night and prayed very long and hard again, for someone to come and save me, or for God to take me. I didn't have a preference; whichever one was to come first was fine by me. I couldn't stand the loneliness and fear any more; it's as if my heart was broken into a million pieces. Everyone has stripped me of my dignity, and what little self worth I had left. I didn't know how much more I could take. Life was too hard.

A few weeks went by. Every single day I would stop at the station and ask if any one called for me. The answer was always the same, "No!"

All of the other girl's mothers or fathers would visit them every week. I was the only one who didn't get a visitor, which made me feel ashamed, worthless and afraid- afraid that I would be in that hellhole forever. I had just about given up all hope.

CHAPTER TWENTY-TWO

A PLACE TO CALL HOME

Visiting day was here. They began announcing names of the girls as their visitors came in. I retreated to the day room. That's where those of us who didn't get any visitors had to stay until visiting hours were over. I was the only one in there most of the time. What I really wanted to do was go to my cell and cry.

Then it happened. They called my name. Not only did I have a visitor, but also the worker said I would be going home. *Home?* I didn't even know where home was. I haven't had a home in so long that I didn't know where I belonged or who I belonged to.

I was so happy to be getting out of there, but what was better than that is someone actually *wanted* me, but whom? I wondered.

I peeked around the corner of the visitor room. I had to squint hard because I had bad eyesight, and couldn't see far away very well. Everything was blurry. I felt excited, as if it was Christmas and I was about to open a gift.

I felt my heart sink. They must have been mistaken because I don't recognize anyone in the visitor room. I should have known better than to get my hopes up. I turned around to walk away when all of a sudden I heard two voices holler at the same time "Susan!" I swung around, and to my amazement I saw my Aunt Tory and her husband, my Uncle Peter. I ran to them and hugged them both so tight. I asked them how they knew where I was, and they said my father told them. They asked me if I wanted to come and live with them. I was so choked up that I couldn't answer- all I could do was cry. I was so relieved and thankful that God had answered my prayers.

I changed into the clothes that I came there with, and left that horrid dungeon with my aunt and uncle. I repeatedly told them for the entire ride home that I couldn't remember ever feeling this relieved or safe in my life. I thanked them and told them I loved them. I felt as if everything was going to be allright.

Aunt Tory and Uncle Peter had two daughters- Lori, which was a little over a year older then me, and Meagan who was only two. They also had three older son's. The boys were made to sleep in the basement on twin beds that were in the boiler room. I felt sorry for them. Lori on the other hand, had a bedroom of her own. It was decorated in pink flowered wallpaper and frilly curtains. She hung posters of rock groups of the day: Deep Purple, Aerosmith, Led Zeppelin and Black Sabbath. Her room was so cool. It was my dream bedroom. Lori also had a lot of clothes. She was gracious enough to share them with me because I didn't have any of my own. She also had a lot of friends in the neighborhood. It was so much fun to be able to go out whenever we wanted to. We all would walk, talk and laugh for hours. Lori didn't have to do any housework and she *never* got hit. This was the closest example to normal that I have ever experienced. I felt blessed to be living there, never the less, I still missed my little sister and brother.

A PLACE TO CALL HOME

There were a few times when I heard my aunt call my mother and father to ask them when they were going to come and visit me. I don't know what their response was but neither of them ever did.

CHAPTER TWENTY-THREE

TWELVE STORIES

This was probably the longest that I've ever been in one school. Lakewood Jr. High made school number four or five (I lost count) in less then two years. I still felt like an outcast, as if I didn't belong. I felt lost and alone but I tried hard to fit in, and enjoy the life I had for the moment because I knew, all too well, that it could change at the drop of a hat.

Lori, the gang and I would walk around the neighborhood most every day. It was a quaint little town by the bay called Lakewood Heights. Mostly middle class people lived there but the people who owned the Victorian mansions on the ocean were rich and considered to be high class. We kids used to sneak down to the beach- it was down a path between one of the houses that didn't have a fence. Everyone went swimming all the time except for me. I would sit on the sand and watch everyone.

When I was very young my uncle and aunt would take us on their boat. They got their kicks out of throwing my sisters, cousins and me off the boat in the middle of the bay and listening to us scream. I was so young that I didn't know that the life jacket I was wearing would keep me afloat. I always thought

A NICKEL IN MY SHOE

I was going to drown or that something under the dark salt water was going to bite, or worse yet, *eat* me. Ever since then, I developed a great fear of the deep, dark ocean.

A whole bunch of us girls went to see the movie "Jaws" when it first came out in the movie theater. When we arrived home, the boys were waiting for us. We all took a walk to the beach and as we were standing on the sand they began to chase us with the intent of throwing us in the water after they caught us. Everyone thought it was fun except for me. I really was screaming bloody murder. Not only did I just finish watching the scariest movie of the decade, but also I had an extreme fear of the ocean-and what lied beneath it, to begin with.

We finally made it back from our walk, or should I say *swim*. It was about 10:45, and my aunt and uncle were still up watching TV. Lori and I sat down with them just as the 11:00 news was about to start. The news reporter came on and said, "The top story of the day…a 16 year old girl jumped out the window of a 12 story building earlier in the evening. The Towers houses low-income elderly people. The unidentified girl landed in a rose bush, arms first, and amazingly enough, is conscious. The cameraman was focused on this girl lying in the middle of the bush. He was asking her what her name was and where she lived, but she didn't answer him. My aunt, uncle, cousin and I watched in amazement, shock and horror, because that girl lying on the ground was my sister Mary. She had attempted to commit suicide by jumping out of my Nana's living room window. Nobody knew about this tragedy yet. Not my mother and not my father. We were the only ones. (*Mary went to visit my grandmother. While there, she asked my grandmother to make her some eggs and toast. While Nana was busy cooking in the kitchen, Mary took the screen off of the window in the living room, climbed up onto the ledge and jumped 12 stories. She landed arms first into a rose bush and through the dirt)*

My aunt, Lori and I immediately left for the hospital, while my uncle frantically searched for my mother and father.

I was experiencing multiple thoughts and feelings simultaneously: sadness, guilt, shock and anxiety. I know I wasn't close to my sister because she was violent and I was afraid of her, but that didn't mean that I didn't love her.

By the time we arrived at the hospital the doctor's had just finished stabilizing Mary in the Emergency Room. We caught up with them as they were wheeling her to the Operating Room. I ran up to her gurney to see her.

Her face and body looked so swollen, and her arms were haphazardly wrapped in (blood soaked) gauze. There weren't any cuts on her face at all. Aside from the swelling she looked normal. I couldn't believe this was happening.

We ran to one of the doctor's, who was running up the hall to catch up with Mary and the nurses. We told him we were her family. He began to tell us, as we were all running, that she was in very critical condition. She had a burst spleen and compound fractures of both arms, as well as severe internal bleeding. He said her prognosis was bleak. We caught up with Mary and they slowed enough for me to tell her I loved her and that I was sorry. Then I kissed her good bye.

I began to cry. I started thinking about all the times I told my mother that Mary was mean to me or Karen and she got hit for it. I, for the first time, felt very selfish because I wasn't the only one who had a difficult life. Mary had as hard of a life as I did- if not harder. I felt guilty for having a home and knowing she didn't. I felt sick to my stomach to think that life was so horrible for my sister that she thought this was her only way out. I may have prayed for death, but I would never attempt to take my own life.

The three of us waited in the family waiting room for what felt like forever. My mother came running in to the waiting area. She was crying. Before someone could tell her what was happening with Mary, my father ran in. He was crying as well. What a crock of shit, I thought to myself. I was so pissed at them both. *Now* they come running.

I was so disgusted and angry with my mother and father that I couldn't look at either of them. I just hung my head. My aunt informed my father of all that the doctor had reported to us, but she didn't say a word to my mother.

Many hours later, one of the surgeons came to tell us that they removed Mary's spleen and stopped the internal bleeding. They had to remove a portion of bones in both of her arms because they were embedded in the dirt after the fall and that Mary will most likely develop osteomyelitis; a severe and potentially fatal bone infection. He warned us that she may need to have portions of her arm bones removed in the future- if she doesn't end up having them amputated.

The doctor informed us that the next twenty-four hours were critical and that if Mary survived, she would be in the hospital for many months. (At least she won't have to worry about having a bed to sleep in or food to eat for a while, I thought to myself.)

Mary began to slowly recover. She had both of her arms in a cast, and received multiple operations on both of them to remove the infected portions of bone- just like the doctor said. She was on potent intravenous antibiotics for many months, but they didn't seem to help get rid of the bone infection. After having the bones in both of her arms amputated inch by inch, her arms looked deformed and were literally like rubber.

TWELVE STORIES

My father would visit Mary in the hospital most everyday, sometimes twice a day-right around meal times. He would eat her food, watch a little TV, and then go to the bar. I don't recall Mary mentioning my mother ever coming to visit her. The crocodile tears that she shed in the waiting room was just another one of her attention seeking performances.

Many months had passed since Mary's suicide attempt and also since I last saw my mother. We were coming up on the fall season. It was my second favorite season. Spring was my first favorite. I loved the fall season because the air was crisp, the colors of the leaves were so vibrant and I loved to watch the squirrels gather their nuts for the winter. Lori knew a lot about nature. She told me that if the squirrels had thin tails, it would be a mild winter and they would leave a lot of the nuts on the ground. If they had a bushy tail, it indicated we were in for a harsh winter, and they would gather every nut they could find.

My aunt and uncle would take us on Sunday drives through New Hampshire to go leave peeping. Lori complained about the long rides because she wanted to be home hanging out with her friends. I would complain too. However, I secretly loved the long Sunday drives, they felt so normal. I imagined it was what *real* families were supposed to do together.

Lori and I were sitting outside in the front yard one day, when the phone rang. I heard my aunt yell, "Susan, it's for you. Your mother's on the phone." I was shocked because I have been at my aunts for many months and this was the first time that she has ever called me.

What could she have wanted after all this time? I wondered. I didn't know what to say when I picked up the phone, so I just asked how Karen and Guy were doing. She said they were fine. I didn't beat around the bush. I asked what she wanted.

A NICKEL IN MY SHOE

My tone of voice was angry. But I had mixed emotions when I heard her voice. I was sad that she didn't want me-and happy because her calling gave me a glimmer of hope. I wanted so badly for her to apologize, *(or at the very least express some sort of regret for putting me in that horrible place)* and tell me she loved and wanted me. I wanted her to tell me that I could come home. She didn't.

CHAPTER TWENTY-FOUR

ABANDONED

My mother asked if she could come and see me on Sunday because she wanted to buy me some new clothes. I told her yes. I was puzzled. Not only did she never call me, but to call me *and* want to take me shopping to buy me new clothes? I didn't know whether to be happy or nervous but what I did know is that something wasn't right.

Finally, Sunday was here. I didn't know what time my mother was coming, I didn't ask her. I pretended not to care, but I did, very much. I think I gave it away when I continually walked over to peek out of the picture window in the living room every *five* minutes or so, give or take a couple of minutes.

Aunt Tory hollered, "Susan, your mother is here!" I intended to make her wait a little bit, so I lingered at the kitchen table where my cousin was sitting. About thirty seconds went by, and I thought to myself, "O.K. that's long enough." I was feeling quite anxious, however, I was trying not to let it show, so I nonchalantly moseyed through the kitchen, into the living room and out the front door.

I stepped into her new minivan and sat beside her in the front seat. I asked where Karen and Guy were, and she said they were at home. My mother didn't look at me at all- she didn't smile at all either. I was wondering why she came to visit me if she wasn't going to be happy to see me. I mean, why bother? So I asked her. While looking straight ahead, with her two hands on the steering wheel, she said, "We are moving."

"Moving?" I asked. "Where?" "Who all is moving?"

She went on to tell me that Fred, Karen, Guy, Mary and her were moving to Colorado.

"What about me, can I go with all of you?" I asked.

"No, you can't," she said- in a flat but nervous voice.

I felt my heart do a tumble salt in my chest. I have felt abandoned many times in my life, but not like that moment. The thought of never see my baby brother and sister again crushed me. I was devastated.

I began to yell at her, "I don't need you to take me clothes shopping just to ease your guilt! You think new clothes are going to make everything all better? You're not even going to let me say goodbye to Karen or Guy? You know what? YOU SUCK!"

Then, something dawned on me, and I lost it, I was completely enraged.

"NOW I GET IT," I said. "You made Nana do your dirty work! You made Nana send me away to that institution for unwanted girls so that you all could move away without me! Didn't you? How could you? You were going to let me sit there and rot forever, weren't you? And look, you can't even look me in my eyes! Why do you love everyone but me? What have I ever done to deserve to be treated less then human all my life? All I've ever done is try to please you and make you happy! I hate you for all that you've done to me! I hate you for taking the people that I love the most away from me forever! I hate you!"

ABANDONED

My mother never said one word in response. She just sat there, clutched the steering wheel and stared straight ahead. She had pursed lips and I could tell she was gritting her teeth. I thought for sure, at that moment, she would backhand me in the face. *(My aunt was watching us out of the window, that's probably the reason why I was so brave, and most likely the reason why she didn't hit me)* I was thoroughly enraged at that moment that I think I may have hit her back. I flew out of the car, slammed the door as hard as I could, ran to Lori's room and crashed onto the bed. I didn't even cry. I had to contain myself because I wanted to break something. I was furious, however, my anger soon turned to sadness, and depression. All I could think of is never seeing my little sister or brother again. I survived worse. I *will* survive this.

Life started to get tough at my aunt's house. She felt sorry for me because my family moved away and months went by without any word from my mother *or* father. My aunt was extra nice to me. She paid extra attention to me and my cousin Lori didn't like it.

My aunt would offer only *me* a candy bar, and *not* Lori. She would tell *me* how pretty I was, but *not* Lori. I didn't have to eat all of my dinner, but Lori did. It was little things like that, which made Lori jealous and resentful toward me. The nice things my aunt did and said to me, and not to Lori, made me feel awkward, but there wasn't anything I could do about it. Those things were beyond my control.

Instead of coming to either me or her mother to explain how she felt left out, Lori displayed her resentment and anger toward me by setting me up to get in trouble.

She first started by giving me the silent treatment. Then she would hang out with her friends and not invite me. They *were her* friends to begin with. I was an outsider. This didn't help her cause because I had nowhere to go and had no friends of my own, so I had to stay with my aunt, which only enhanced our relationship, and brought us closer.

My cousin no longer allowed me to wear any of her clothes. She said, "You're wrecking them, and besides- *my* mother and father get *paid* for you to live here, tell them to buy you your *own* clothes." She made sure to make me aware of *my place* in *her* home.

When my aunt asked me why I was wearing the same outfit everyday, I told her it was because it was the only outfit I owned. I surmised my aunt spoke to Lori about the clothes, and not inviting me out anymore because Lori began to ignore me as if I wasn't even there. My cousin was not used to getting spoken too- she was quite spoiled.

My cousin invited me out the next day to hang out with her friends. I was relieved. I figured she and my aunt had a heart to heart talk and that Lori wasn't mad at me anymore. We were hanging out on the street that led to the beach when everyone started talking about how much fun it would be to pull a fire alarm. Everyone was urging me to pull it. They all told me that it was cool to watch the firemen look for a fire, and how they all have done it before- except for me. I told them over and over again that I didn't want to do it because I felt it was wrong and I didn't want to get in trouble. They wouldn't stop badgering me! They said I wouldn't get in trouble because nothing was wrong with it, and they wouldn't tell anyone if I didn't want them too. They continued to badger me- all the while making it sound exciting.

I always felt that I didn't belong and that they all were borrowed friends. I thought maybe if I pulled the fire alarm they would accept me as a true friend. I knew in my heart pulling the alarm was wrong, but more than that I wanted to be accepted- I wanted so desperately to fit in.

I pulled it! Everyone began to run in all different directions. I stood there wondering why everyone was running because they said it was fun, and that there was nothing wrong with it. As they were running they all began hollering at me, they were yelling things like...

"I can't believe you did that!"

You're gonna be in soooo much trouble!"

"You're so stupid!" "We were only kidding, you idiot!"

I yelled *"WHAT?"* "All of you talked me into it! You all said it was fun and that there wasn't anything wrong with it! You tricked me!!!" They adamantly denied saying any of it- straight to my face. I didn't realize what was going on, however, it didn't take me long to figure out that it was a set up. My cousin wanted to make her mother dislike me as much as *she* did. She wanted to show her mother that I wasn't the perfect little angel she made me out to be. Lori used me so that she would look better in her mother's eyes. I was condemned for things I had no control over.

I ran home. I thought for sure that Lori would stick up for me since she also encouraged me to pull the alarm. I was wrong.

My aunt, uncle and Lori were standing there waiting for me. They looked like a firing squad minus the rifles. My aunt and uncle were standing there with their hands on their hips, while my cousin stood there-she had her arms crossed and an evil smirk on her face. My uncle pointed in my face and asked me, "Susan, now don't you lie to me, did you pull that fire alarm?" There was such disappointment in his voice mixed with anger. I felt so disappointed in myself for letting them down after all they have done for me. I didn't know what to say. I looked at Lori, thinking she would speak up and defend me, but she didn't.

"Yes uncle, I did, and I'm sorry," I said.

My aunt asked me why I did that after all the kids told me not to. I turned to look at Lori. If my facial expressions said what I was thinking they would have said, 'you liar, you evil spoiled rotten bitch!'

My uncle said I've been causing a lot of hard feelings between my aunt and cousin, and now I was getting in trouble with the law. So they said it was best that I leave. I glanced over at Lori. She had a slight smile on her face, and she turned away so that no one would see her laughing.

She set me up. She ran home to tell her mother the exact opposite of what *really* happened. I turned to my cousin and said, "You win, I hope you're happy."

My aunt found my father and told him that my mother split town. She said they could no longer care for me. She told him he *had* to take me. He said he couldn't because he had no place to live either. He told my aunt to call the Connor's and ask if I could live there until he found someone to live with.

That's what my aunt did; she called the Connor's to ask if they would take me. Mrs. Conner told my aunt to call the state social worker to make the necessary arrangements.

CHAPTER TWENTY-FIVE

THE BIG BLOW

My life was an emotional roller coaster. I lived with the Connor's for the next year. Nothing changed. We had to "sneak" food to eat, they whipped their kids daily, and we hardly ever went to school because we were either too tired from cleaning the house all night, or just because we weren't allowed to go- same old story, different year.

My mother called the Connor's. She told them that she was moving back home and needed to see me. She had something important to tell me. She told the Connor's the *big secret*, but they wouldn't tell me. By the look on their faces, it wasn't good.

I was on eggshells for the next two weeks. That's when I was supposed to meet with my mother. I wasn't sure of the day, but I assumed she'd notify me.

There was a knock at the door. It was my mother. She asked me to come and sit in her van with her. It was an awkward few minutes because neither of us spoke. I didn't ask how or where anybody was and I didn't ask why they moved home. It's not that I didn't care- it was because I was tired of being the *only* one to ever make an effort to start a conversation or to have a relationship.

She broke the silence by saying, "I missed you." I asked in amazement, "You did?" My heart began to melt. However, I was skeptical. I told her I missed her and everybody as well. Then the big blow came.

"I came here to tell you that Nana has lung cancer, and she only has a few months left to live."

I felt the floor drop out from under my feet. It felt, for a split second, as if someone had electrocuted my heart and at the same time, felt a rush of heat flow through my face, head and body. I became dizzy, light headed and a wave of loneliness and despair rippled through my soul.

"NO!" I screamed. "Nana *can't* die, she can't leave me, I can't live without her- if *she* dies *I* will die. My heart hurts, it's crumbling!" I clutched my chest and bent over. I checked to see if my hands had blood on them because it felt like my heart was actually bleeding. My mother grabbed me and hugged me, but I pushed her away. It was too late.

I was sobbing so hard that I told my mother I was going to throw up. I rolled down the window and hung my head outside. When I was finished vomiting, and through my sobs, I told her to pick me up as soon as she could because I needed to be with Nana. She said she would.

I went to my room and cried, and dry heaved all night long. I didn't get out of bed for over a week. I know I have suffered sadness in my life, but I have never felt a feeling such as this before-monumental devastation and grief, as well as profound sorrow.

Mrs. Connor didn't know what to do with me or for me. I overheard her telling Mr. Connor that she was afraid I would hurt myself, and she was going to call my mother because she wasn't going to be responsible if I did.

THE BIG BLOW

Call my mother? That surprised me, because she *despised* my mother. The feeling was mutual between them. My mother and Mrs. Connor were "the pot that called the kettle black," so to speak. They were both equally guilty of the behavior that they condemned each other for. I didn't understand why they couldn't see, or didn't know, what they both were doing to their children was criminal.

After all that I have been through in my fourteen years of life, I have always been able to rise above the abuse, loss, bullying, and what ever else came my way. I was able to pick myself up, dust myself off, and learn to laugh and at least appear on the outside, happy again-but I couldn't this time; I couldn't seem to recover.

After receiving the news of my grandmothers' terminal illness, I couldn't snap out of my depression. I had not one ounce of motivation. I couldn't eat. I couldn't sleep, and at times I couldn't stay awake. I felt as if my heart had been torn out of my chest, and I just couldn't rise above the heartache and anguish. I felt as if I was too weary to fight anymore. My life had been an up hill battle, filled with disappointment and pain for as far back as I could remember, and I couldn't deal with it any longer. I sat the Connor's down and told them I needed to live with my mother so that I could be with Nana.

"I need to spend every last possible second with her before she died," I told them. "I love you both very much, but this was something I had to do for my grandmother as well as for myself."

They said they understood, and that I could come back to them if things didn't work out. I thanked them, and gave them a hug and kiss.

A NICKEL IN MY SHOE

Deep in my heart I knew I'd be back with the Connor's one day. I came to realize by now that moving in with my mother wouldn't be permanent. I just never wanted to believe it. It was hard, day after day, to watch the kids be tortured by their mother and step-father, but to me, that was normal. That's all I knew, because it's all that I saw and experienced all of my life. I thought all parents in all households treated their children this way. You only know what you see-even though you know what you're seeing is wrong.

I had always hoped someone would be brave enough to report the Connor's for the abuse and torture of their children. All of the teachers knew what was going on in that house-they had to. Mrs. Connor made no attempt (that *I* was aware of) to hide the bruises *when* she sent them to school. Everyone who should have cared-didn't. They all turned their backs, and had a blind eye. Each and every one of the Connor children, just like me, were swept under the carpet and forgotten about. I'm not surprised that all the other transients that periodically lived in the house didn't report them-they needed her because they were down and out-they weren't about to bite the hand that was feeding them, besides, everyone was afraid of Mrs. Connor. She was someone to be very afraid of if you made her mad. This was a woman that *nobody* dared to cross.

I had made this decision on my own. My mother didn't even know about it yet. However, there is one thing that I *was* sure of and that is I wasn't going to take no for an answer. I was determined that <u>NO ONE</u> was going to keep me from my grandmother. I called my mother and explained why I needed to be with Nana, and told her if she didn't pick me up I would walk the twenty miles it took to get there. She complied, and why wouldn't she? She needed a *'slave'* now more then ever- because that's all I ever was to her.

My mother, Fred, Karen, Guy and Mary, along with Nana, rented a small apartment just outside of the city. It had two bedrooms, a living room, a kitchenette and a dining area. Nana had the master bedroom while my mother, Fred and baby Guy slept in the second bedroom. The rest of us slept in the living room.

Life wasn't easy. I was surprised to find that there was hardly any food in the house. Guy was dirty, and my mother and Fred weren't getting along too well. I surmised the reason was because he wouldn't pay the rent, and when he did it was two weeks late. It was very embarrassing to open up the front door everyday, only to find an eviction notice attached to it. We were the only family in the complex who couldn't enjoy the pool because my mother and Fred never paid the rent on time, if at all. Not that I would benefit from it, but it would sure save me a lot of embarrassment.

Nana was so sick. When my mother gave her morphine injections, she would vomit twenty minutes later. She was in so much pain all the time. I would lie in bed beside her and rub her back. She said it helped to relax her but I think she was just being polite. I didn't know what to do for her-I felt so helpless.

Often, I would take my brother for a walk around the complex. I stayed away from the kids that would hang out in back of the recreation hall after it closed every night because I knew they were smoking pot and I didn't want to expose my brother to anything bad. I was happy that they never tried to force me to smoke with them. They would offer for me to go with them, and when I declined, they would laugh and say, "good, more for us." That was a relief.

A NICKEL IN MY SHOE

Almost everyday, while Nana was taking a nap, I would sit on my front steps hoping that a boy I knew would come by and visit me. He lived up the street and his name was Anthony-he was so adorable and I liked him so much. I would make any excuse that I could to take my brother for a walk just to sit and talk with him. Anthony was quiet and shy around other people-but not with me. We would sit on my steps and talk -mostly about music. I never wanted our time together to end. Aside from taking care of my grandmother, Anthony gave me motivation and a reason to look forward to another day.

One afternoon, while taking my brother for a walk around the complex, I spotted some of the kids down by the tennis courts. I started to walk in their direction. When they saw my brother and I they began yelling. "Hey, there's Guy with the eyes!" They came running toward us. As usual, they talked about the color and beauty of his eyes for the first five or ten minutes. They asked me why we haven't been around the complex, and where we've been. I explained how sick my grandmother was with cancer, and how I needed to rub her back every night because she was in so much pain.

One of the kids began telling me that he was reading how smoking pot takes away cancer pain, and that I should give my grandmother a joint to smoke.

"What, are you crazy?!" I said. "Are you trying to get me arrested?"

"No, honest," he said. "It's been proven to relieve pain in cancer patients."

"Thanks, but no thanks," I said. "How would I ever pull *that one* off?"

THE BIG BLOW

As time went on, Nana's pain got worse. My mother was constantly giving her injections of the morphine, plus codeine pills. My mother would cry every time she injected Nana because she knew she was hurting her. She was constantly vomiting now, and she would cry and moan from the pain. The doctor's said the cancer was traveling to Nana's bones and brain, and it wouldn't be much longer before she died.

I was desperate to ease my grandmother's pain. I told my mother I was taking my brother for a walk. This was the only reason that she'd let me out of the house. I met up with the boy who told me about the studies on marijuana and how it reduced the pain of cancer patients, I told him I was considering getting a joint for my grandmother. I told him how much pain she was in and that the pain medication made her vomit. He told me that smoking pot would help with the nausea as well. That's it, my mind was made up. I decided to take the chance. I've never broken the law- not on purpose anyway, but it was for a good cause. I asked him if he would give me a joint. He said he would give me the first one, and if it worked and I wanted more, he would charge me a dollar a joint.

It *did* cross my mind that if I got caught, I would go to jail. Never the less, easing Nana's pain and suffering was more important to me. I decided that I would gladly go to jail if it meant reducing her suffering. I met my friend behind the recreation hall and he gave me the joint.

I felt very strange, as if the police were going to come screeching around the corner and arrest me! I had to get that thought out of my head. I had to keep reminding myself that this was something I *had* to do for my grandmother.

Nana was so naïve- there was such an innocence about her. If there was one thing she always made me do, it was smile.

We were lying in bed that very night when I broached the subject of pain. I started by asking her to what length she would go to in order to ease her pain.

"Oh Susan," she replied. "I hurt so badly that I'd do *anything* to take my pain away."

I asked her if she remembered the times that she would sneak me cigarettes, and ask me not to tell my mother.

"Yes," she said. "I remember, and I'm so sorry. Please Susan, please stop smoking," she begged. I ignored her plea. It was too late for me to stop smoking and I wasn't going to make a promise that I wasn't sure I could keep.

I told her that I kept my promise, and never told my mother. I went on to ask her to make the same promise to me- not to tell my mother what I was about to tell her.

"I promise, right hand to God, cross my heart, that our conversation would be our secret," she said.

I began by telling her that I had a special cigarette that was made especially to ease pain and nausea, and that would make her eat and sleep better. The look on her face was one of astonishment. I continued to tell her that these cigarettes were illegal in the United States, so she couldn't tell a soul if I were to give her one. Nana gave me her word.

At that moment, my mother came through the door to give Nana her shot. I gave her a kiss, told her I'd return to rub her back after I gave Guy a bath and put him to bed. She winked at me, and I left the room.

Later, when I was rubbing my grandmother's back while she was vomiting, she told me how desperate she was to smoke the special cigarette. I stressed to her that since the cigarette had a strong odor, we would have to wait for my mother to go someplace where she would be out of the house for an extended period of time. I also told Nana that she would have to smoke the cigarette by the bedroom window. She agreed.

The next day, before my mother left to visit her girl friend in the city, and go to a doctor's appointment, she gave Nana her injection. She left me instructions that she could have two of her pain pills in a couple of hours, only if she needed them. I asked my mother when she'd be back and she said she should return in three or four hours.

As soon as my mother walked out the door I heard Nana holler for me.

"Susan, get me the bucket, I'm going to throw up…hurry!" I ran into her room, scooped up the bucket off the floor and held it under her mouth. I rubbed her back while she was vomiting, and dry heaving. I couldn't take it any longer. Any doubt that I had about doing this illegal thing faded away. I was 100% sure that I was willing to accept any consequence that was thrown at me if I got caught. I didn't even care at this point if my mother walked through the door.

After Nana was finished, she laid there moaning and telling me she didn't know how much more she could tolerate. I told her that it was time to smoke the special cigarette. I helped her out of bed, and walked her over to the chair I had placed in front of the bedroom window.

I got the joint, lit it up and handed it to her. I told her to smoke as much of it as she could. She began to puff on it. She complained that it was too strong, and it burned her throat. She said it was making her dizzy and light headed. I told her all of that was normal.

Nana put the joint out after smoking only half of it. I helped her back to bed and told her to just relax and let the medicine in the cigarette take effect. While she was resting, I opened all of the windows in the house and sprayed all of the rooms with perfume. I went back to check on her and she was snoring! I was so happy that she was finally getting some rest and that it actually worked. Nana slept for two hours straight. That was more than she had slept straight in over three months. When she woke up she told me she was hungry, and asked me to make her something to eat. I made her some chicken noodle soup with bread, and a cup of tea. It was the first meal my grandmother had kept down in many months and she didn't ask for her break through pain medication that day. I found a miracle. I bought more marijuana and she smoked every chance she got.

Nana passed away two months later. She progressively became weaker, and incoherent. Then came the time when she woke up in the middle of the night screaming that monsters were trying to stab her. When we all entered her room she was flailing about as if to fight the 'monsters' away. We realized the cancer had attacked her brain. We were telling her it would be all right, and how much we loved her. We all helped in getting her dressed and my mother and Fred took her to the hospital, where she died later that night. I didn't know that would be the last time I would see my grandmother. Although my heart was broken and I wanted her to live forever, I was thankful that I was able to help ease her pain and suffering, the best way I knew how- toward the end of her life.

I felt as if my world fell apart that night. This earth was an emptier place and I felt like an emptier person. I never missed someone so much in my life as I did my grandmother. I never experienced someone close to me dying before, and didn't realize the finality of it. I couldn't get it through my head or my heart that I'd never see her again, at least on this earth. I would look for her face in the crowd everywhere I went. I didn't want to believe she was gone forever. Her death was surreal. She always told me that we'd meet again in heaven one day. God, how I longed for her. I felt as if my security blanket was torn away from me. I didn't feel safe in this world without Nana.

The house became eerily quiet with my grandmother gone. My mother slipped into a dark depression. If I thought there was no food in the house, and she neglected my brother before, it was *nothing* compared to after her mother passed away.

CHAPTER TWENTY-SIX

JUST LET ME GO

Fred and my mother began to fight more often- usually over money and bills. They finally split up and Fred moved out. Life was very tough because there was no money coming in at all and my mother was going out all the time-almost nightly.

My mother borrowed money from a friend so that we could move into the apartment below the one we were already living in- because it was cheaper. It had only one bedroom so whoever fell asleep in it first won. The cupboards were practically bare, not because my mother didn't want to buy food- she just had no money for food. She had to go to the state and apply for welfare. The small amount of food stamps she received, however, didn't seem enough to feed all of us for very long. We had to go without food for extended periods of time, until the next check came in. We made sure that Guy always had something to eat and Karen worked hard to get invited over friend's houses for dinner so that she could try to bring left-over food home for Guy and I. Mary was hardly ever there, so not having any food in the house didn't matter to her. She was often with her new "weirdo" boyfriend, Brian. He always acted the same way Nana did after she was through smoking a joint.

A NICKEL IN MY SHOE

Brian had light brown curly hair, and squinty, half opened eyes. He was very thin, and disheveled looking. Every time he came over I wanted to toss him a bar of soap and a can of deodorant. I wondered what Mary was doing with him because she was an overly clean person. She was forever in the bathtub. She longed for a shower, but couldn't take one because she had casts on her arms. I would help her place plastic bags with rubber bands over her casts when she bathed, which was three times a day, and I would (or someone would) have to wash her hair for her over the kitchen sink.

Brian drove a beat up old motorcycle. I didn't like it when Mary went with him on it. I always thought that motorcycles were too dangerous, and he appeared to be a dim whit. I didn't trust him- my instincts told me not to.

Mary was in the tub when the doorbell rang. I opened the door and Brian came stumbling in. It dawned on me that this kid was high. I asked him if he was on drugs. He tried his best to respond, but I didn't understand one word of his slurred chatter.

It was summer time and very warm in our apartment. We couldn't afford to turn the air conditioner on so Brian, very clumsily, removed his jean jacket. To my astonishment, his arms were covered in bruises and track marks. *Oh my God!* I thought to myself. I thought he was smoking dope, but no, he shoots heroin! Now Mary *really* isn't getting on the bike with him!

I told him to leave the apartment or I was going to call the cops. I also told him to leave my sister alone-or else. He stumbled out the door and departed on his bike. Ten minutes later, Mary came walking out of the bathroom and into the closet in the master bedroom. While she was fishing for something to wear, she told me to send Brian into the bedroom. I told her he was high. She said he always was high. I slammed the door shut, and locked her in. I told her that I sent him home, and it was for her own good. She was irate.

"Let me the fuck outta here!" she screamed. "I'm gonna fuckin *KILL* you, you sonofabitch! You wait, I'm gonna kill you..."over and over again. I truly was afraid for my life, and was praying that my mother would walk through the door. For the next hour, Mary continued to bang on the door and threaten my life. Mary and I have had quite a few fist fights, and one of us would end up dead if no one was around to break us up. I know it would be me, because Mary had the strength of an ox and she was impossible to hurt.

My mother (brother and sister) *finally* came home! I told my mother what had happened. She said I did the right thing. I told her Mary was going to kill me, and that's exactly what she attempted to do after my mother 'freed' her from the closet. She lunged at me, slamming her casts into my head. My mother was trying to pry her off of me but was having a hard time doing so. After my mother succeeded, I got up on my feet, my mother was holding Mary away from me, but not far enough. Her foot came up and kicked me square in the stomach. I thought I was going to suffocate to death. I couldn't breath. She knocked the wind right out of me. I was gasping for air, but couldn't get any. Finally, in what seemed like forever, I started to breath. I truly thought I was going to die. While my mother was screaming at us both, Mary took off out the front door. I didn't regret what I did. I actually felt relieved that Mary was safe, even though I caught a beating for it.

Later that night, I was watching the 11:00 o'clock news with my mother, and who do we see wrapped around a tree?

Brian. After leaving our house that day, he drove to the park and hit a tree at an estimated 60 miles an hour. I turned to my mother and said, "Oh my God. Mary would have been on the back of that bike!"

Mary returned home the next day. She didn't speak to me all day. She seemed more distant then ever. I broke the silence by asking her if she knew about Brian, she said "yes."

"You would have been on the back of that bike you know," I said.

"I know," she responded. "You should have let me go. I hate you."

Mary's behavior was stranger then ever. I had a sneaking suspicion that she was a drug addict as well. She didn't take her lithium because my mother couldn't afford it; therefore, Mary was spiraling downward, mentally as well as physically. Infection continued to plague the bones in her arms, and she was continually in and out of the hospital to have her bones removed, inch-by-inch. When Mary wasn't in the hospital, she was with her druggie friends.

CHAPTER TWENTY-SEVEN

THE MIDDLE OF NOWHERE

Out of desperation, I'm sure, my mother and Fred got back together, and we all moved to a house in the country. There wasn't a store for miles, and the people that lived in the near by shacks were unusual. They all looked slightly deformed, like they were inbred or something. Karen told me when she slept over her friend's house, her father would wait until he thought everyone was asleep, tip toe into the bedroom and force the little girl to go to his bedroom. She told Karen he does that with all of her sisters and that it was "her turn."

We lived in an old farmhouse that had rickety floorboards and squeaky stairs. I didn't like it. That house gave me the creeps. No matter how my mother tried to brighten it up, it always was dull and dingy. My mother started to change at this time. She began to complain about physical ailments that had no cause. If her head didn't hurt, her leg did. If her stomach didn't hurt, her back did. It was constant. She was becoming a hypochondriac and there was a '*miracle* pill' for every ailment she complained about.

She claimed to have hurt her back, but didn't know how she hurt it. She just woke up that way. She had a traction (orthopedic) bed set up in a room located off of the kitchen. She lay there 24/7, and expected me to wait on her hand and foot. This included assisting her with the bedpan. She claimed she couldn't even get up to use the toilet. I was stuck cleaning that entire miserable house, doing all the wretched laundry and taking care of the baby…24/7, while Karen got to go out with her friends and play- all summer long.

There was a lake in back of our house. You couldn't see it because it was about a quarter mile down a long winding path that ran through the woods. While I was being held prisoner and slave (that's what I felt like), I could hear all the laughter while the neighborhood kids were jumping off the tire into the lake, and just having a good time. I longed to be with them, swimming and having fun.

I swept and washed the floors, cleaned the bathrooms from top to bottom, washed the walls, cleaned the windows took out the garbage, dusted the furniture, cooked all the meals, took total care of the baby and my mother…everything my *mother* should have been doing. And if she really couldn't, the entire family should have contributed, but they didn't. This was all too familiar. So, one day I told her I wasn't going to do all of the work all by myself anymore.

She called my stepfather's sister to come over to scold me. She was a disheveled woman who lived like a dirty pig. I think that she would be considered a hoarder by today's standards. She had some nerve coming over to my spotless house, and giving me hell about giving my mother a "hard time" concerning cleaning. I was sweeping the floor when she walked in. She began to yell at me, saying things like, "You're a lousy daughter. How could you be so lazy, with your mother lying there sick? How dare you give her a hard time? If you were my daughter, I would beat the shit out of you!" I could tell that she was putting on a show for my mother, who lay there in the next room listening to every word. I told her that she lived like, and was a pig, and that if my house wasn't clean enough for her then she could clean it herself. Then, I threw the broom at her. She began to swear at me, told my mother I was a spoiled brat that needed a good beating and stormed out the door.

Later on, after my step-father came home from work, out of spite, my mother hobbled out of bed, sat at the table, roughly placed Guy on the table in front of her, picked up a spoonful of baby food and *shoved* it down his throat. His head flew backward and he began to choke. I became enraged.

I ran over, grabbed my brother from off of the table, and patted his back until he could breathe again. I began to *scream* at her, "How dare you treat that baby so rough! Who do you think you are to get up out of that bed after two months and shove a spoon down that baby's throat! I'm not going to allow you to hurt him like you've hurt me!"

My stepfather came running out of the pantry, and started screaming at me.

"That's *his* fuckin' mother," he shouted, "That's who *she* is!"

"You could have *fuckin'* fooled me!" I screamed back. "I thought *I* was his mother. *I'm* the one who is raising him, not *you* and not *her*! I am the *wife* around here, not her!"

He ran right up in my face and raised his fist. My mother sat there and didn't say one word. I said,

"Go ahead, fuckin hit me you pig," I blurted. "I'll tell my father and he will *KILL* you!"

"GET OUT," they both screamed at me. "GET OUT NOW!"

A NICKEL IN MY SHOE

Fred grabbed me by my hair and tossed me out the front door in the dark and middle of nowhere, in my nightgown. I didn't know what to do, or where to go. What I did know is that I was afraid for my baby brother.

I didn't know which way to go because I didn't know where I was. There were no street lights- the only light I had to guide me was moon light. To the left of me were woods, and to the right of me the same for as far as my eyes could see. I didn't know anyone nor have any friends that I could run to because I was never allowed out of the house. I walked for miles, (hoping I was going in the right direction to 'civilization') until the sun came up. I was so scared. I thought someone was going to kidnap me. Every time a car drove by I would hide behind a tree or in the bushes by the side of the road until it went by. I *finally* came to a gas station that had a pay phone. *Thank God,* I thought to myself. I was entirely exhausted, mentally as well as physically, and don't think I could have made it much farther without collapsing. I called the Connor's collect. I was crying. I told them what had happened. I was in my nightgown and I was so scared and embarrassed. Once again, they came to rescue me.

Mrs. Conner asked me why I kept going back with my mother. I told her that I didn't know the reason why. I guess I was always hoping she'd change. I was always wishing she'd one day love me and treat me like a *real* daughter. I never lost faith that someday my wishes would come true. With every time I moved back in with her I'd say to myself; this is going to be the time that she will give me a big hug and kiss and tell me she's sorry. This is the time that she'll let me go out and meet, and hang out with kids in the neighborhood, and maybe even have a friend sleep over…maybe this will be the time…

CHAPTER TWENTY-EIGHT

AN ENEMY WITHIN

Almost a year had passed. Life at the Connor's remained the same. I was starting to feel like a prisoner. I wasn't allowed to grow and become independent. I was almost sixteen-years-old, and *still* was not allowed out of the house-neither were any of the Connor kids for that matter. I was becoming interested in boys, but that was a huge no-no. Dating wasn't allowed, *ever.*

I began to change. I felt that if I didn't break free soon I would burst. I wanted more out of life, such as an education. I wanted so much to have the opportunity to become a nurse and someday have a family of my own. But there was no way to achieve my goals if I was a prisoner. Every one in my life did with me what was best for them. No one seemed to have my best interest at heart. I would have been happy just to be allowed to have a mind of my own or to be allowed to form my own opinions and actually have them valued.

In order to survive in the Connor's house, you had to tell them what *they* wanted to hear or there was hell to pay- the price for *all* of us kids was sleep depravation due to being forced to clean the house all night long. For the rest of the kids, it was beatings with the cat o' nine tails whip or being thrown in the clothes dryer and tumbled around for a while. I longed to be my own person, and to have a normal life, what ever *that* was.

My father came to pick me up a little more often these days. It seemed as if he was slowing down now that he was getting older. He was now living with a woman named Jeanie. They were planning on getting married soon, and that surprised me because she was not at all my fathers' type. She was heavy set and taller then my father. She had beautiful red hair and kind eyes. Jeanie had a nervous, high-pitched giggle that was utterly annoying, but her cheerful personality made up for it. She was a happy go lucky woman, except for when it came to her son, Gregory, who was six-years-old. He was adorable, with light brown wavy hair, and big brown eyes. She never spoke to him in a normal tone of voice, she screamed at him instead:

"GREGORY, TAKE A BATH! PICK UP YOUR CLOTHES! EAT YOUR DINNER! PICK UP YOUR TOYS! GET OVER HERE...DO THIS, DO THAT!"

When the little boy didn't obey her *immediately,* she would take him in the bedroom and beat him. I felt so sorry for him because I knew first hand what that felt like; pain, humiliation, and terror. What was sometimes worse than that was the 'wonder', (wondering why you were getting beat when you didn't do anything wrong.)

Jeanie and I got along very well- we laughed and joked around a lot together. She was more like my sister then my stepmother. I was happy that my father found a stable woman who didn't have a drinking problem, and I thought I could ever so subtly help Gregory. I felt that there was finally hope for my father. She kept him under her thumb, but he also seemed content to be more settled down. He would go out periodically, but when he did, he wouldn't stay away from home for days on end like he used to. He would go to the bar and come home when it closed. There was another thing I was noticing about my father- he was losing weight. Every time I saw him he looked thinner.

My father informed me that Jeanie was pregnant. I felt so excited- If there is one thing I couldn't get enough of in my life it was babies. I begged them to please let me live with them. I made a pitch that I wanted to go to school, which was something that has been scant in my life since the age of eleven. I also told them I wanted to get a job- yet another thing I couldn't do because of the constraints of the Connor's. Jeanie happily agreed.

Visiting Jeanie and my father once a month or so turned out to be very different then living with them. There were some rules that I didn't like at all. The worst one was that I was only allowed to take a bath twice a week—on Sunday and Wednesday, and I could only fill the bathtub up three inches.

On nights when Jeanie wasn't home, which wasn't very often, I would sneak a bath and fill the bathtub half way up. That felt like pure luxury. The one thing I liked the very most is that I had a lot of freedom. I could visit friends and they could visit me. Jeanie gave me a curfew of midnight on the weekends, and I used up every minute of it!

My father was much more lenient. My girlfriends and I would meet him at the bar and he would sneak us a bottle of Amaretto, or we would meet him at the city nightclub and he would buy us drinks. I wasn't eighteen yet so it was the same routine every week- the bouncer would ask me for my ID and every week I made up an excuse as to why I didn't have it with me. One weekend the bouncer told me if I didn't bring my license the following week he wouldn't let me in. I had to get creative, so I dug out Nana's license. I had it in my saving box along with her glasses and Rosary. The following week, when the bouncer's asked for my ID, I handed him Nana's driver's license. Well, I thought he was going to pee his pants laughing. The bouncer went running to show his buddies. Needless to say, they let me in and never carded me again.

I was very excited to be back in school. I was in eleventh grade, and much to my surprise, was never held back. I took this as a compliment at the time. However, the school system did to me what everyone else has done to me all of my life. That was not care, turned their heads, sweep me under the rug, and push me along until they were rid of me.

My Uncle Steven was a computer programmer for a large city hospital. He was kind of a 'big wig', and he helped me to get a job after school, in the medical records department. He set up an interview for me with the old woman who supervised that department. When I went in for the interview I took one look at her and wanted to burst out laughing. She had one thick, gray and untamed eyebrow that ran straight across her forehead. She also had a mustache that was thicker and longer then my father's was! Every time she spoke to me the tips of her mustache would wiggle, and I would have to hold my breath in order to not burst out in to laughter. I had the biggest smile on my face throughout the entire interview. She must have thought I was a *very* happy person.

Life was good. I had a new baby sister. Her name was Tara and she resembled my sister Mary. She was plump and had a head full of thick dark hair, unlike my sister's and I when we were newborn. My father said we looked like scrawny, bald monkeys.

AN ENEMY WITHIN

Finally, for once in my life, I was getting up everyday and going to school. I was determined to succeed but it was a struggle because I had missed so much for so many years. After school I would take the school bus home, change my clothes then take the city bus to work. On slow nights at work I would do my homework. On busy nights I wasn't able to complete my assignments, and had to stay in detention during my school lunch break. I didn't mind because I was so tired everyday that it gave me a chance to catch a catnap.

I was getting by in school with mostly C's, and a couple of D's. I just couldn't catch onto the math. Every other subject wasn't so hard to punt my way through because it was just a matter of memorizing the book, or my notes, but math was exact. Finding the *time* and the *energy* to do the work and reading was the *real* challenge.

Every night, when I came home from school, my baby sister would speed crawl to me. She would put her arms out for me to pick her up and give her a million kisses. It was the same routine every night; I would bend over, take a hold of both of her legs and swing her, as if she was sitting on a swing at the park. She giggled and laughed the whole time. She hated when I had to let her down but I needed to eat and get ready for work. She cried for me to pick her up until I left the house.

Jeanie spoiled Tara with lots of hugs and kisses. She had so much patience with her. I wished she had the same patients with Gregory. While living there, I would sneak in his room and clean up the toys. I would tell him to take a bath and get in his pajamas so that he wouldn't get in trouble. Jeanie saw how much I loved both of the kids, which appeared to have worked in Gregory's favor; she seemed to go easier on him. I couldn't believe it was almost Tara's first birthday. Time was sure flying by.

I was pretty excited to find out that my father was going to pick Karen up this particular weekend. I haven't seen her in so long, I missed her so much. I tried to call her a few times, but my mother wouldn't let her come to the phone. This was the only way she could punish me. This was the only control over me that she had left.

Karen was quiet as usual. She told me that my mother and Fred got divorced and that she had a new boyfriend. Karen said they went out drinking a lot and she had to stay home alone. I didn't like hearing this, so I told her that if it was okay with my mother, I would baby-sit for her on weekend nights. Karen seemed to like that idea. She told me she missed me very much and she was lonely without me. I felt the very same way.

Karen played with Tara, and we took a lot of pictures that day. I'm so glad we did because those were the last pictures I would ever take with my father.

CHAPTER TWENTY-NINE

MISS YOU DAD

It was the beginning of January1979, and my father was losing weight like crazy. He began to complain everyday of slight stomach pain. However, he was too stubborn to go to see a doctor. He hardly got up out of bed anymore.

A few weeks back, I had met Steven at a nightclub. He was three years older than me and very handsome. He was tall with blonde hair and blue eyes. But I wasn't sure that I liked him all that much. There wasn't any chemistry between us. Also, there was something about him that made me feel uncomfortable, and I couldn't figure out what it was. On one hand I was flattered that an older boy liked me, and on the other I think that's what scared me. He asked if I would go with him and two other couples to a New Years Eve party in Canada, and also to a hockey game. The first thought that ran through my head was that my father would kill me, but I said yes anyway.

After I said yes to him, fear rippled through my body. I was so scared. I was sure Steven expected me to have sex with him. I knew I didn't like him enough for *that*. I was afraid to have sex. I heard what it sounded like, and it sounded violent- like it hurt too much. Besides, it was too embarrassing. I thought if he liked me enough he would understand. My biggest dilemma was how to tell my father that I was going away with a boy. That was an even bigger fear!

One Friday night, as I was getting ready to go out with my girlfriends, my father called me in to his room. I lay down beside him.

"Susan," he said. "I want to tell you I love you."

"I love you too Dad," I replied. Then I said "There is something I have to tell you, but I don't want you to get mad at me and hit me. You have to promise.

"Are you pregnant?" he asked.

"OF COURSE NOT!"

"Then what is it?"

"I met a boy, and he invited me to go to a party in Canada next weekend for New Years. The next day we're going to see a hockey game."

He paused for a minute before speaking; "Susan, I need to tell you something- I need to tell you that I'm going to die, and it's going to be soon."

"DAD!" I cried. "THAT'S NOT FAIR! YOU'RE JUST MAKING THAT UP SO I DON'T GO AWAY WITH A BOY! THAT'S A TERRIBLE THING TO SAY!" I jumped out of the bed, gave him a kiss on his cheek, and told him it was a nice try, but I *was* going with Steven to Canada.

Unfortunately, the trip didn't go over so well. We hopped a plane, and went to a hotel. After checking into our room, I made it clear that I wouldn't sleep with him. He didn't speak to me for the rest of the trip except to say that I was a waste of his money and time. That's when I knew I made the right decision! It was the most tension filled two days I've ever spent with anyone in my life. I just wanted to go home- I only wanted to be with my father.

Wow, Tara's birthday was next week, I thought to myself. I couldn't believe she was going to be one-year-old. It felt as if she was just born. I walked in to my father's room to kiss him goodbye before leaving for work.

"Susan," he said. "I don't feel good. I'm having trouble breathing and I feel like I'm going to throw up. Get me a bucket." By the time I got back with the bucket, he had run to the bathroom to vomit. While he was bending over the toilet, I noticed just how thin and frail he had become. What he told me kept ringing through my head over and over again, "Susan, I'm going to die, and it's going to be soon."

He was vomiting up what looked like coffee grounds. I didn't know it then but he was vomiting up blood. I screamed for Jeanie to call the ambulance.

After my father was admitted to the hospital, the doctor's told us he had internal bleeding, but they couldn't find where it was coming from. I went to visit him one day after school. He told me he was having trouble breathing, and the pain in his stomach was getting worse. I asked the nurse to put oxygen on him, but she refused saying she didn't have an order for oxygen. I became extremely irritated and angry. I told her to get her lazy fat ass on the phone with the doctor, and if oxygen wasn't on him in five minutes I was going to call a lawyer. My father had oxygen on in less than three minutes. I sat with him for a while, and begged him not to die. I told him that I couldn't live without him. He told me I'd have to.

Jeanie walked in a few minutes later. She made the mistake of telling my father that Tara had taken her first steps.

A NICKEL IN MY SHOE

He began to rip the blankets off of himself, and said he was coming home to see Tara walk. We begged him not to, but there was no reasoning with him. It was now January 15, 1979.

My father made it home to see Tara walk, but that very night he was profusely vomiting up blood. Jeanie called the ambulance to have him taken to the teaching hospital in the city, the same one I worked at. I received a call while I was working and was told that my father was admitted, and was asked to come up to his room.

I ran as fast as I could. I scolded him for leaving the other hospital, but told him I understood why he did. I told him I wouldn't leave him, and how much I loved him. I fell asleep in the chair beside his bed that night. Sometime in the middle of the night a team of nurses and doctors ran in- abruptly waking me as they surrounded my father. They began to frantically shove tubes up his nose and down his throat-there was so much commotion in the room. I just stood in the corner in shock. My father was starting to turn yellow and was in a coma. He never woke up again.

Seven days had passed and I *never* left my father's side. I talked to him all day, and held his hand all night. He had turned completely dark yellow in a week's time. The nurses were complaining that I smelled very bad and that I needed to go home and take a shower. They were right. Jeanie said she would drive me home so I could take a bath. I told my father that I would only be gone for a little while. I kissed his cheek, told him I loved him then hugged him and said goodbye. It only took ten minutes to get home. When we walked through the front door the phone was already ringing. I thought it was the hospital calling to tell me my father woke up, and he wanted me to come right back. But, on the other end of the phone was my father's doctor telling us that he had expired. I didn't know it then but someone in the family gave their consent to turn off my fathers' life support.

I didn't want to believe my father was gone. I had to go back to the hospital to see him just one last time. I ran into his room- he looked so peaceful. I kissed and hugged him- I didn't want to let him go. I told him I would love and miss him forever- and that I would never forget him. The date was January 22, 1979- the most devastating day of my young life.

CHAPTER THIRTY

YEAR OF NUMBNESS

The loss I felt was tremendous. I was beside myself with grief and sharp pains surged my heart. It felt as if my heart was bleeding. I didn't know where to run or who to turn to. I called my father's brother to come over just so I could look at him because he resembled my father. I would sit beside him on the couch and cry my eyes out. What I was feeling was beyond explainable; it was a combination of shock, fear, grief, devastation and a feeling of utter loneliness and despair.

For the next week I ate Jeanie's Valium like it was candy. I wanted to sleep my life away. I would wake up in a panic and Jeanie would give me Valium so I would fall back to sleep, I couldn't deal with the reality of my father's death.

I felt so empty and numb- like a zombie. I didn't feel love, hate…nothing, except for profound grief, and I didn't know how to deal with it. I just couldn't cope. I started drinking heavily, smoking pot and exhibiting reckless behavior, such as staying out all night long, getting so drunk that I could have easily been taken advantage of- raped, kidnapped, beat up or even murdered. I started missing work, and I didn't even care. I didn't care about me or anybody else. I was tired of life. I was tired of the disappointments that slammed me one after the other. I couldn't seem to catch a break and I couldn't handle it any more. My fathers' death was the icing on the cake.

Jeanie's personality and demeanor changed soon after my father died. She wasn't nice anymore. She became strict and mean. She sat me down and told me that I wasn't her daughter, and if I wanted to continue to live there that I would have to pay her $50.00 a week.

I didn't make $50.00 a week, and I could only work 20 hours because I went to school full time. I would have to work full time, if not some overtime in order to give her the amount of money she demanded!

I tried so hard to work full time and keep up with school. I was too skinny to begin with and started to lose even more weight because there was no time to eat. My grades plummeted from mid C's and D's to D's and (mostly) F's because I fell asleep in class everyday. I couldn't keep up with that schedule any longer. I cried as I resigned from high school. My father would have been so disappointed, not with me, but with Jeanie.

I worked the night shift and if Jeanie wasn't home to let me in the house after I returned home from work, I would have to wait on the hallway stairs until she returned home. I had to listen to the young couple that lived upstairs fight and argue for hours on end. I was so exhausted all the time. I needed to get sleep before going to work, and sometimes I wasn't able to because she would come home too late. She refused to give me a key, and when I argued that I was paying rent and should have a key, her come back was, "Well, you can move out if you don't like it, you know."

I told her that's exactly what I would do. I didn't care if I slept on a park bench, because I didn't care about my life, or what happened to me. I only wanted my father back. Nothing else mattered anymore- so I thought.

My cousin Maria lived not too far away from Jeanie. She was one of my Uncle Ray's daughters. Maria was newly married and had two little babies. I knew she didn't have much money and thought she could use some extra, so I broached the subject of me moving in with her in exchange for weekly rent. She thought it was a great idea.

I quit the medical records job to get better hours at a nursing home and worked as a nurse's aide on the 3-11 shift. The nursing home was located in an extremely crime ridden part of the city. I had to walk through side streets, and back alleyways to catch the bus to and from work. It was scary, but I had no choice. Being on my own, I did what I had to do to survive.

Working the 3-11 shift at the nursing home was so much better than the 11-7 shift in the medical records department at the hospital. It felt so unnatural to stay up all night long. I longed for my comfy couch every night, so I was thrilled to find a job with better hours, as well as in a field where I could be truly helping people that couldn't help themselves. It gave me a sense of self worth because before working at this job I had none.

The people that worked at the nursing home were mostly African American. I was one of the very few Caucasian people- aside from most of the licensed nurses, that is. Everyone seemed nice enough however everyone, for the most part, kept to themselves.

The work was hard, and no one ever offered to help anyone else. Hell, they didn't even want to do their own work. It was my turn to take out the trash. I hated this task because I had to walk down the back stairwell, which was dimly lit, dark and eerie. I went to gather the trash that the nurses' aides had thrown in a heap under a window that faces the front of the building. I glanced out the window as I was bending to pick up a bag and I saw a huge black man dragging a bleached blond white woman across the street by her hair while she kicked and screamed. He was heading toward our building, and began to round the corner, which was direction of the back of our building, where the dumpsters were located.

I took off running to the nurse's station. I ran up to the head nurse and told her about what I had just witnessed. She said,"girl, you best mind your business, or he'll be draggin' you back there."

"What?" I said. "You're not going to help her?" You're not going to call the police?" *(Nurses aids weren't allowed behind the nurse's station to use the phone)*

"Of course not!" she replied. "You don't get involved in street matters, it's none of our business, and you'll do best to keep your nose clean! Now smarten' up and go to work."

I could hear all the other aides laughing at my naivety. I asked if anyone would be willing to go with me to throw the trash out (since they were only watching TV anyway), and they laughed even louder, saying, "You're on your own girl." My heart sank at that moment; on my own, that's the story of my life, why should tonight be any different.

As I was carrying the garbage down the stairs I could hear muffled sounds coming from beyond the exit door. I put my ear to the thick metal and heard a man yelling and a woman screaming. She was talking rapidly *and* she was crying-both at the same time. I could only imagine what was going on out there. My heart was pounding. I wanted to help her so badly, but I knew if I went out there alone I would be in danger, and wouldn't be able to do anything for her, being alone and all. I waited there until I didn't hear any more voices or noises. I was sure hoping someone would come and help me throw out the trash, but no one did. Roughly 20 minutes went by. I slowly opened the door and peeked outside. There was a streetlight that lit up the back of the building. The man and women were gone and all I could see was the dumpster with garbage strewn all over the ground. The coast was clear, however, I was still afraid to go out there all by myself.

I had about fifteen trash bags to carry. I picked up the first three and, reluctantly, began to exit the building. That's when I saw something beside the dumpster that looked like a head with blonde as well as red matted hair. I tiptoed around the side of the dumpster to find that the blonde girl was slumped over; she was covered with blood and barely recognizable as a human being. Her eyes were half open. They were staring straight ahead. Her mouth was open as well.

I said in a low voice, "Hey, hey are you alright? Are you awake?"

She didn't respond. I think she was dead. At that moment it felt as if my heart dropped to my feet. I turned around and ran back in to the building and notified the nurse supervisor. She rolled her eyes in her head and picked up the phone to call the police, while mumbling under her breath.

When the police arrived they asked for my statement. I told them exactly what I saw, which wasn't much because it was too dark outside- and what I had heard, again, not being much because the metal door was too thick to hear words through, I could only hear muffled sounds.

The woman turned out to be a prostitute as well as a drug addict, a dead one at that. I was appalled at the fact that no one wanted to get involved to help this poor girl. If only the police were notified sooner, she may have survived the brutal attack that she endured.

I always knew this particular area was exceptionally dangerous, but seeing the brutality with my own eyes made me realize that my own safety was in jeopardy every time I walked out that door at 11:00 at night. Taking the mile walk through the side streets and alleyways, to wait for the bus home now petrified me.

CHAPTER THIRTY-ONE

INNOCENCE LOST

It was a cold and rainy night. I was dreading the walk to the bus stop. The bus was late picking me up for work at 2:30, and I got drenched waiting for it. I couldn't seem to get warm. I had the chills all night at work. The only way to get rid of that kind of bone chilling cold was to take a nice hot bath.

The nurse supervisor informed me that one of my patient's bed needed changing. I gathered my linens, and went into the room. I normally spoke to my patient's while changing them, however, I wasn't feeling well this particular evening, and remained quiet. All of a sudden, a nurses aide named Yula, walked in to the room I was working in and asked me if I needed help. I thought this was *extremely* strange, because no one *ever* helped anyone else, even when asked.

Yula was a very unattractive African American girl. She was tall and lanky. Her eyes bulged out of her head and her complexion was blotchy, with dark and light spots from her forehead to her neck. There were large dark freckles mixed in with pimples that covered her cheeks as well. She always looked tired, and 'used up'. She was quiet and seemed nice enough. Yula mainly kept to her self. We worked together on the same unit for about three months but she never spoke to me unless it was work related and absolutely necessary- even then she never spoke more then a sentence. I couldn't figure her out. She appeared depressed, scared, angry, stuck up, and sad, all wrapped in one. She always looked the saddest when she came in to work, and right before it was time to go home. I never gave it much thought though, I was too focused on trying to make it to the bus stop without getting mugged, raped or killed.

Yula walked around to the other side of the bed. We weren't supposed to hold conversations with each other while changing a patient. *All* of our attention was to be on *that* patient, and rightfully so. However, this patient had extreme dementia and didn't understand anyway, so I saw no harm in talking to Yula while working, just this once. I was actually very happy that she asked if she could help me. I was even more excited that she wanted to be my friend.

I told her that I would most certainly appreciate her help. She started to help me roll the patient so that we could strip the sheets from underneath her. Yula was very quiet at first, and then she asked me, "Hey, do you party?" I said, of course I do, I go to parties. She became silent again. I began to wonder what she was trying to get at, and then she said "would you like to go to a party with me and my friend sometime?" I said, sure! We finished changing the patient then left the room.

It was my turn to take out the trash again and as I was gathering all of it up, Yula said, "Hey, let me help you." I looked around the room because I wasn't sure that she was speaking to *me*. She said, "Yeah, I'm talking to you Sue. Do you want my help?" I said, sure, thanks!

Yula grabbed a few bags, and I grabbed a few bags and we both headed for the back stairwell. She became quiet again and it made me feel very uncomfortable, so I tried to make small talk. I told her how I hated to take the garbage out all by myself and how coming down the back stairwell gave me the creeps, especially after the murder that took place out there. She continued to remain quiet. We got to the next landing and she dropped her bags of trash and leaned up against the wall. I stopped as well, and asked her if she was allright. She said she was tired and wanted a little rest. I didn't understand why she was tired when all we did was walk down *one* flight of stairs. After a brief silence, she began to make conversation, however, she appeared nervous, and the conversation sounded forced and rehearsed. She said "yeah, I have to work two jobs, but I get to keep the money from *this* job…to support my son. The money from my other job goes to my boyfriend." I asked her what her other job was, and she said she "hustled." I felt like an idiot because I didn't know what *hustled* meant. I figured it meant that she sold drugs. I pretended to not let what she said shock and scare me, but it did. If I was sure of one thing in my life it's that I didn't want to hang out, or be friends with people who dealt drugs, but I felt like it was too late for me to back out now.

Yula said, "Girl, you must be afraid to walk to that bus stop bein' so late at night en' all," I said, you bet I am! It's *real* scary walking down the alleyway between Elmwood and Broad Street. She asked "how'd you like a ride home tonight? My friend said he'd be glad to give you one, you know, since it's rainin' en all." I said that I would appreciate, and be relieved to get a ride home. I felt so thankful that I didn't have to walk down the alley on such a rainy and cold night. I told her thanks, and then we continued down the stairwell to throw the trash away. She became quiet again.

A NICKEL IN MY SHOE

There was a black Thunderbird waiting out side for Yula and me. It had very dark tinted windows and all the chrome lining the sides of the car and the wheels were polished to perfection and had such a high shine that the car seemed to glow in the dark.

Yula seemed to be in much better spirits, as well as relieved when our shift was finished, and it was time to go home. I thought maybe she took a liking to me and was worried about my safety while walking to the bus stop every night, being in such a dangerous neighborhood and all. It felt nice to have a friend who cared about me. All my friends seemed to only care about themselves. They didn't have the worries that I had. Their parents provided a home, food, a bed- and their parents *wanted* them. They didn't have to worry about paying rent, eating, or even *if* they'd have a home or parents tomorrow. All my friends had to worry about were things like; when's the next party or school dance- and rightfully so.

Yula opened up the passenger side door and a plume of thick smoke rushed out of the car and hit me in the face-my eyes immediately began to water and sting. I began to feel somewhat uneasy at that point. I couldn't see in to the car yet because I was standing up. "Get into the front seat," she said. "No," I replied, "That's okay, I'll get in the back seat." She snapped and said, "NO, I *said* get in to the front seat." I didn't know how to take her harsh but nervous tone of voice. I was a little bit bewildered, and felt somewhat apprehensive, but I said okay, and got in as I was *ordered* to, after Yula climbed in to the back seat.

"Susan this is Rhett," she said, introducing us.

"Hi, nice to meet you." I said.

INNOCENCE LOST

Rhett was an African American man, with much darker than average skin color. I could tell that he was very tall, and slightly over weight. He had his left hand on the steering wheel as he leaned to the right, at the same time resting his right elbow on the middle compartment as he toked on a joint. The entire car was filled with smoke. The thick smoke immediately went up my nose and down my throat, and I wanted to choke, but didn't dare. I pretended that it didn't bother me. He made a gesture as to hand me the joint. "No, thank you," I told him. "I don't smoke pot anymore. I don't like the effect it has on me."

I felt awkward because no one spoke once we got in to the car. Rhett was sizing me up, looking at me from my head to my toes, and back again. This made me a little nervous and self-conscious. I was wondering what he was thinking.

I had just turned seventeen years old. Everyone told me I resembled Susan Dey from the Partridge family and sometimes younger kids would actually ask for my autograph. I had long dark wavy hair, light brown eyes, and wore too much make-up, however, we were approaching the 1980's, and that was the beginning of the era of 'big hair' and wearing heavy make-up. I had a nice shape- so I was told. Being petite at 5'4" and 100 pounds earned me unwanted attention from boys my own age, as well as from men that were twice my age- but I wanted *NOTHING* to do with them. Men scared me.

"So, Yula tells me you like to party," Rhett said.

"Yeah," I replied. "I go to parties all the time." I didn't tell the whole truth- I didn't go to parties *all* the time, just once in a while, and they usually busted up early because a parent would come home and ruin the fun.

Rhett made me feel awkward. He continued to tilt his head, you know, like a confused dog would do. And after asking a question, he would then bob his head, which reminded me of the plastic dog my mother used to have sitting in the back window of her car. The dog's head would bob after riding over the bumps in the road.

He then asked me if I might be interested in meeting a few of his friends. He said that he knew someone that would be interested in having sex with me. I said, sure, I'd like to meet some new friends, but I couldn't have sex with anyone. He asked me, "Why not, you gotta disease?" I just laughed a nervously, and said no, it's not that at all! I can't do that because I'm a virgin. I want my first time to be special if you know what I mean. His head started to bob faster, and the grin on his face widened.

"Yeah," he said. "I know zactly whatchoo mean. I'm looking forward to partying with *you* girl."

I was so glad that he understood where I was coming from and he *still* wanted to be my friend, even though I refused to have sex with his friend. He was polite, in a quiet and eerie sought of way, but I thought he was harmless enough. He drove me back to Marie's house. I thanked him, and told him it was nice meeting him, then exited the car. A feeling of security came over me. I felt as if I didn't have to be afraid anymore because Rhett was my friend. He had an air of power about him. I felt as long as Rhett was on my side I didn't have to fear anyone.

The next day rolled around. It was a sunny spring day. Winter was finally ending. I was so tired of the cold weather and snow. I was definitely looking forward to the grass turning green, the spring tulips, and most of all, hearing the birds singing when I wake up in the morning.

INNOCENCE LOST

The phone rang, as I was getting ready to leave for work. It was Yula asking me if I wanted a ride to work. I happily accepted. I began to tell Marie, very briefly, about my new friends.

"Susan," she said. "I don't have a good feeling about this. Please take the bus and be safe."

I said, "Be safe? Hello...earth to Marie...do I need to remind you that we live in one of the most crime ridden and dangerous neighborhoods in this state? Do you even have a clue as to know what it feels like to have to walk down side streets and alleyways twice a day? It's the scariest thing anyone would have to do even once in his or her lifetime. I have to do it twice a day, EVERY DAY OF MY LIFE! So, when someone offers me a ride, I'm taken' it!!! How much more dangerous can taking a ride from a co-worker be then walking in a dangerous part of town late at night?"

I heard a horn beeping out side of the house. When I looked out the window and saw Rhett's car, I yelled to Marie that my ride was here.

"Oh, Susan, please, I wish you wouldn't," she said. I told her to stop worrying about me and that everything would be fine. I gave her a kiss on her cheek and ran down the stairs and toward the car.

The car windows were as dark in the daytime as they were at night. I tried to peer through the tinted glass before opening the passenger side door, but couldn't see in. I opened the door, jumped in to the front seat and closed the door. I immediately turned around to say hello to Yula, but she wasn't there. Rhett pushed a button and I heard both his and my door lock. I felt a rush of heat that started from the top of my head and flowed quickly to the bottom of my feet, and at the same I felt a little 'zing' in my heart, as if a volt of electricity shot through it. I have felt this feeling many times in my life, and it was always when something very bad either happened or was about to happen to either Karen or me. There was only one thought that entered my mind, and that was, *"Oh my God, I'm going to die today, and in one of the most horrible ways one could ever imagine."*

I asked him where Yula was, but he didn't answer my question. He said he was taking me down the street to the drug store to meet his friends. He wasn't smiling or bobbing his head today. He had a very serious and cocky look on his face. I wondered what had happened to the nice man I met last night. Then it all clicked. I was tricked and now I knew that I had to fight fire with fire and trick *him* if I was going to make it out of this situation alive.

I couldn't think straight. The drug store was only a few blocks away. I had to think of something fast, my life depended on it. Rhett pulled in to a parking space that faced the main road. I was frantically searching the street for a police officer, but it dawned on me that even if I spotted one he wouldn't be able to see me through the tinted windows. My heart sank. I was on my own. I felt utterly doomed.

Rhett noticed that I was eyeing the door handle and lock.

"I see what you're looking at woman," he said. "Don't even think about it. That would be a good way to fuckin piss me off, and that's something you don't even want to try little white girl, besides, it won't open anyways." That was the only time I saw him smile, but it wasn't a friendly smile, it was a fiendish and evil smile.

All of a sudden, I saw two, absolutely huge, black men exit the drug store. They were walking our way! I felt all the blood rush from my face, and my heart began to pound so hard I could see my uniform shirt moving in and out to the beat of it. My head began to tingle and I started to feel faint. I started to, ever so quietly, hyperventilate.

Rhett rolled down the window and the two men bent down and poked their head in. They were so big, mean and dirty looking. I thought I was going to lose consciousness right there and then. They both began to speak at the same time, saying, "Oooowhey, and dam! She is FINE! "What a cute young thang, I can't wait to get my hands on her…girl you so fine, you gonna make us alotta dough." Rhett turned his head to look at me, he began smirking and bobbing his head, just as he was doing the night before. My head was swirling with thoughts of how to get out of this alive. I needed another "nickel in my shoe."

Suddenly it dawned on me…what Yula said…she's allowed to keep the money from the nursing home to support her son and what she makes on the street must go to (what I realized to be) her pimp- Rhett. At the same time I was thinking this, one of the men told Rhett they couldn't meet with us right now because the other (third) person was out on *business.* But, they could meet with us later on that night.

I started to ramble in the most enthusiastic voice I could muster. Trying not to sound nervous, I said "You know Rhett, I've been doing a lot of thinking since last night. I realized that I could make us a lot of money. I can imagine buying tons of furs and diamonds- maybe even a Cadillac…oh yeah, that's the stuff *I* always wanted. We could all share it together- not to mention I make some pretty decent money at the nursing home. But the only thing is- they told me if I was late one more time they were going to fire me, and it's almost 3:00 now, we'll have to hurry. I can't get fired because I would lose way too much money. They pay me a lot there, you know!"

A NICKEL IN MY SHOE

They were all listening to me with smiles on their faces, and of course, Rhett was bobbing his head up and down like a jerk. If I could read their faces and type of smile, it would read something like this: "What a stupid bitch- she thinks she's going to get to keep the money she makes out on the street. The only thing she's keepin' is half a paycheck from wiping ass and a needle in her arm."

"So," Rhett asked. "You *will* be able to meet our new friends later, right?

"Oh, yeah, and party I hope," I said.

He started to smile with that same "stupid bitch" look on his face that he had a minute ago. He said, "Yeah, there's gonna be a party all right." Then he turned to the two guys and they all burst out in to laughter. "Oh no!" I said. "I only have 10 minutes to get to work, we have to leave now or I'm fired! I said, nice to meet you guys, I'll see you after work!"

Rhett didn't say a word for the entire ride there. I could tell he was in deep thought. Finally he broke the silence by giving me an order- as if he *owned* me. "I'll pick you up at 11:00. Don't be late, we have business waiting."

"I won't be late, I can't wait to meet everyone, see you after work!"

I ran in the front door of the nursing home and slammed my back in to the wall because my legs were giving out- I fell to my knees. My entire body was shaking. I was trying to breathe into my hands because I was getting dizzy from hyper-ventilating. I was so sick to my stomach and was trying desperately not to vomit.

I sat there for some time. As the fear subsided, anger began to take over and I became furious. I don't ever remember feeling this angry in my entire life. It was an extremely frightening feeling. When I felt strong enough to finally be able to walk, I got back up on my feet and ran to my unit to find Yula.

I found her in the TV room writing in a chart. She looked up at me and her already big eyes grew to what seemed like the size of saucers-there was a fear in them that was shocking.

"Oh no, I thought you were with Rhett!" she yelled. I ran up to her, took hold of her hair and dragged her to the back stairwell and down one flight of stairs. I grabbed her and held her up against the cement wall. I began to scream at her, asking how she could do such a terrible thing to me-or any human being for that matter.

"If you don't go with them, they are going to *kill* me!" she cried. "Why should I care about what happens to you-you certainly didn't care about what happened to me! "I asked her what they were planning to do to me *exactly.* Yula didn't want to answer me at first, but I threatened to call the police- only then did she begin to (reluctantly) tell me the horrifying truth.

"They were going to take you to a motel room, where a bunch of men and women would be," she said. "Then they were going to tie you up, gang rape and beat you because that's what they do to "prime" the girls they lure in- too show them who is boss." She added, "Then they were going to shoot you up with heroin, so that you would be dependant upon them. You see, if you're an addict then you will willingly prostitute yourself, which makes Rhett's job easier. You wouldn't go runnin' to the cops or nothin'- because you would be doing something illegal too. Look, if you don't do this they *will kill* me, he told me so."

I told her I didn't care what they did to her and that she deserved what ever she had coming to her for what she did to me. She betrayed my trust, and took advantage of naivety and innocence. I was in shock. I let her go and walked away.

A NICKEL IN MY SHOE

Yula began to trail behind me while begging and pleading for me not to leave and for me to meet Rhett after work or she was going to die. I ignored her. I promised myself that I wouldn't use the term 'friend' so loosely anymore. People were going to have to *earn* my friendship and trust, from that point forward.

I walked out the door, all the way down the side street and through the alleyway with my head held high. For the first time in my entire life I wasn't afraid. I felt as if I could survive anything. I felt as if something was missing, or maybe it was more of a feeling as if I had *lost* something-I felt hollow. I couldn't put my finger on it exactly. I knew one thing for sure and that was I trusted *no one* any more. I felt as this was the day I grew up. This was the day I lost my innocence. I felt as if my father and Nana were both watching over me and protected me from harm that day.

I miss them both so much. It makes my heart ache till this very day- thirty plus years later. At that time it seemed that the people I loved the very most died. I was becoming afraid to love anyone anymore, so I started to shut down my emotions and push away the people that I loved the most, such as Karen and Guy. That way I couldn't be hurt, and they would be safe as well.

I took the bus back to Marie's house. I explained everything that happened. She agreed that I was lucky to be alive. She was also kind enough to not say, "I told you so." Both of us agreed that it was definitely not safe for me to continue living in that neighborhood because Rhett would be very angry and soon come looking for me. I, once again, packed my bag and Maria's husband, Benny, gave me a ride to the Connor's. As usual, they welcomed me with open arms.

CHAPTER THIRTY-TWO

FOREVER ERIC

While living at the Connor's, out of the clear blue Mary calls me. I haven't seen her since my father's funeral, and can't remember when I saw her before that. I barely remember my fathers' funeral because I took so many Valiums that week to try to numb the pain. What little I remember of my sister, however, is that she gained a ton of weight. I don't remember speaking to her at all. I may have, but again, I don't have much recollection of that day. I was in a world all my own. That's the beauty of that particular drug…it helps one to forget.

I was shocked to hear from her, and even more shocked that she found me. Mary and I lived like a couple of nomads. We moved around so much we wouldn't be able to keep track of one another's whereabouts even if we tried.

I asked her how she found me, and she said she called Jeannie, who told her I was staying with Maria. In turn, Maria told her that I had moved back in with the Connor's.

I asked her if she was all right. She said she was fine and that she was pregnant- with a boy. After hearing that news a profound sadness came over me. I suddenly felt a sense of doom for her unborn son. I couldn't even choke out the word *'congratulations.'*

I asked her if she was going to keep the baby or give him up for adoption. She was insulted and became belligerent. I didn't mean to offend her by any means. It was just that she had zero patients, a short fuse and a terrible temper. She lost all self-control when she became angry. I knew her baby would be in terrible danger. I also wondered how she was going to afford to provide the basic necessities that a baby requires on a disability and small welfare check. This situation was dismal. I asked her who the father was. She told me his name, but I don't recall what it was now,-Mark, Steven, or Brian, I think, anyway, it was a one-night stand, and they didn't mean anything to each other.

Mary asked if I would come and stay with her until the baby was born. He was due in April. My birthday is April 18, so I was hoping he would be born on my birthday, of course. I thought to my self, *live with her? I'm afraid to be in her presence for more then an hour, never mind live with her!* But then I thought of what she would do to that baby if I didn't, and that scared me to my core.

I can see it now. The baby awake and crying all night. Instead of rocking or walking and soothing the baby, she would whack him or worse yet, kill him.

"Yes," I said. I decided that I would stay with her and help raise her baby. I told the Connor's that this was only temporary and I would be back. I needed to buy some time to try to figure out what I was going to do to keep my nephew safe.

I moved in with Mary on a cold rainy night. I was so depressed. I felt so sorry for this little unborn baby, knowing he would be in for a life of abuse, but not if I could help it, I thought. I planned on taking it one day at a time. I would try not to give her any reason to be angry with me so that I could stay long enough to ensure the baby's safety.

FOREVER ERIC

Mary's house was in a seedy part of town. It certainly wasn't a place that I would want to raise a child. I had high hopes for my child. That is if I was lucky enough to have one someday. I actually wanted four kids, but if God wanted to bless me with one, I would be thankful. I knew what kind of mother I wanted to be, and what kind of mother I didn't want to be. I also knew I wanted to marry someone totally opposite of my father— a non-drinker, or at the very least a man who only drank socially on rare occasions, a non-womanizer, someone with a sense of responsibility and a steady job. I wanted to marry someone that loved as well as respected me-and above all, someone who would be a good father. That's right, I wanted it all, and I wouldn't settle for anyone, or anything less.

How sad, I thought to myself. Mary lived in a slum apartment building. There were roaches in the cupboards and everything was extremely outdated, dull, dingy and filthy. The only furniture in the two-room apartment was a built in dresser and a tiny table with two worn out chairs.

I asked where her bed was. She said she didn't have one, and that she slept on the floor. I was appalled. Mary was seven months pregnant and had to sleep on the floor, she must have been so uncomfortable. My heart broke for her.

"Susan," she said. "C'mon, it's no big deal." I'm not spoiled like that and neither are you. Can you remember the last time that you actually slept in a bed?"

"No," I said. "But I'm not pregnant either! I told her that I was going to make sure she ate right, and was going to be as comfortable as I could afford her to be. I told her that I had one more paycheck coming to me from a job that I had to quit abruptly, and I would spend it on the baby and food. I even got up the nerve to call my mother and ask if she would help out in any way she could. She told me she was very afraid of Mary, but she would buy the baby a cradle. She felt the same way I did. We both were very sad for the baby.

The nursing home owed me one more two-week paycheck, and I owed them an explanation and an apology. I hopped the bus one day that week to pick up my last paycheck. I went in to the office to retrieve it and to tell them what happened. They told me that after that day, no one has seen or heard from Yula again and that Yula's family was still looking for her. I told the secretary exactly what Yula had told me about her being killed if I didn't meet her pimp boyfriend after work that night. I also said that I could give a shit less what she did with the information that I just told her.

I went to the bank, cashed my check, and took the next bus to a department store that sold discounted clothing, food and household goods. I had so much fun. I bought diapers, infant gowns, and t-shirts, booties a sheet and blankets as well as some baby formula and cereal. It was all I could do to carry it all. I had a long walk to the bus stop so I asked the woman to double bag all my items.

Mary was excited about the baby clothes. It took a lot to make her smile, and this did. It made me happy to see her happy. We took a walk to the launder mat and washed all the baby clothes. That was the very first fun time we ever had together in our whole lives. This was one other of the very few memories in my life that I will treasure.

Nighttime was a different story. I didn't sleep very well while living with Mary. It wasn't because we had to sleep on the floor, heck, I was used to that. It was because Mary would, and could snap at the drop of a hat for no reason at all. I needed to sleep with one eye open or the voices might tell her to hurt or kill me in the middle of the night.

FOREVER ERIC

Karen, Mary, and I were driving by the Providence River. I was driving (Jeannie's car), Karen was sitting beside me and Mary was in the back seat. We were cruising along, and listening to the radio when Mary piped up and said,

"Hey Susan."

"What?" I said.

"The voices are telling me to stab you in the back."

"WHAT?"

"You heard me, they are telling me to stab you in the back."

Karen was looking at me with a look of astonishment on her face. I screeched the car to a halt then threw some loose change at her and told her to get out of the car and take the bus to where ever she was going. I knew she couldn't help her sickness but she sometimes did what the voices told her to do. For Christ sake, they told her to jump out of a twelve-story window and she did! She told me that the voices are so loud she does things just to "shut them up." My mother couldn't let Mary move back in with her for the same reasons- the voices and the threats. No one is safe around her. That was why I needed to stay with her- to keep this baby safe.

One of my former junior high school teachers had become a lawyer. I called him and told him about my situation and how I was afraid the hospital social worker would take my nephew away once he was born. He gave me some wonderful advice, starting with getting a full time job, and proving to the court that I was a responsible adult so that I may be emancipated. He also suggested we move out of the slum and back in to the Connor's house. It was in a better neighborhood and there were other people around to help with the baby. I didn't tell him about the abuse that the Connor children suffered on a daily basis, but they never physically abused me and it would only be a temporary arrangement.

I suggested to Mary that we move in to the Connor's house so that the baby would be in a safer neighborhood. I didn't dare tell her about the conversation between the lawyer and myself. She would have became paranoid and taken it out of context.

I explained to the Connors that I needed to find work so that I could help support the new baby. I didn't ask them, I told them. I found a job as a nurse's aide roughly about 15 miles away from their house. I had to walk about a mile and a half to the first bus stop, then about another mile to the next bus stop. I was determined to take my lawyers advice so that the state wouldn't take my nephew away. After about a month or so of steady work, I applied to the courts for emancipation. The court date was set. I appeared with the social worker and my lawyer that vouched for me as being an upstanding and responsible person. I proved to him that I had a full time job and promised to enroll in a program to obtain my GED. The judge granted me emancipation. He said I had every right an adult had except that I couldn't drink alcohol. I was now an adult in the eyes of the court. However, in the eyes of the Connor's, I was still seventeen.

It was Mary's' birthday, March 26. She woke up and said she was having cramps. I told her it couldn't be labor pains because it was too early to have the baby. She said that she thought she was in labor. I told her it was wishful thinking because it was her birthday. She said she was going to visit a few friends that day, and she left the house.

Later on that night the phone rang. I picked it up and it was Mary. She said she was in the hospital and that she had the baby. I said; you're kidding me. I'm not falling for that.

FOREVER ERIC

"No, really," she said. "Listen." She held the phone out and I heard a newborn baby whining. "Oh my God!" I said. Hey everybody, Mary had the baby! We all piled in the car and headed to the hospital. I was so excited. I was an aunt! I couldn't wait to see him and hold him!

We arrived at the hospital and took the elevator up to the maternity ward. All of the babies were in their bassinettes- in back of the glass window. There were so many of them. I looked for his name; Eric Eugene…there he was. He was so tiny and so very cute. I fell in love immediately. I couldn't wait to give him his first hug and kiss. The nurses were doing rounds at each bassinet. The babies were crying so loudly that the nurses had to talk over them, therefore you could hear everything they were saying about each baby The nurses then stopped at Eric's bassinet. I could hear them talking about Mary and her psychiatric issues. I was so embarrassed and at the same time scared. One nurse kept rolling her eyes in disgust, and I'm not sure if I heard correctly but I think she said she wasn't sure if this baby was going home with his mother. I became very afraid that they weren't going to let Eric come home.

I immediately ran to the nurse's station. I told the charge nurse who I was and that I needed to see the hospital social worker as soon as possible. She was peering at me strangely then she picked up the phone and called her. The nurse told me she would be up within an hour. I told her that I would be visiting with Mary, and that I wanted to speak with her privately, without my sister present, when she arrived.

The Connor family was still at the glass looking at all the babies. I headed to Mary's room. She was lying in bed when I walked in. I went up to her, hugged her, said congratulations, and told her how beautiful Eric was.

She didn't say anything to me, at least for the first five minutes. I asked her what was wrong. She remained silent. Finally, she broke the silence.

"I have no feelings for him," she said.

"What did you say? I asked.

"You heard me. I have no feelings for him. I know I'm supposed to love him but I don't. I don't 'not' love him either. I just don't have any feelings."

"I'm sorry, Mary. Don't beat yourself up. I heard that is normal, and will come in time." I told her.

"Really?" Mary asked.

"Yes, really," I said. I was lying through my teeth! I never heard of such a thing in my entire life, but I needed to say something to help her feel better and ease her guilt. I didn't want my sister to start to resent her son.

"Mary," I said, "there is something I need to talk to you about, but you have to promise not to get mad or take anything I say the wrong way.

"I promise," she said. I began to tell her that there is a good possibility that they won't let the baby come home with her because of her illness. She conveyed to me that it wasn't a shock to her and she half expected that. I told her that the social worker was coming to speak with me, and to let me handle things and do all the talking. She agreed.

Mary rang the call bell. A nurse asked her what she wanted. Mary asked her to bring the baby to the room. I was afraid at that point. I knew when I held this baby that I would fall head over heals in love with him, and if we were not able to take him home I would be devastated, and don't think I could handle another huge loss.

The nurse wheeled the baby in.

FOREVER ERIC

I couldn't resist. "Can I hold him," I asked.

"Of course," she said. I picked him up. He was just a tiny little guy. I cuddled him and made a wish. It was a different but simple wish- that he would be *safe* with his mother. I kissed him and hugged him, and cried for him. I felt so sorry that he was born into such terrible circumstances. I whispered to him that I loved him and I promised to never let anyone hurt him.

The social worker poked her head in the door. I invited her in to Mary's room. "You wanted to see me, in private?"

"We can talk in front of Mary," I said.

The social worker was a cute little old lady with white curly hair. She looked very sweet and wasn't intimidating. That was good!

I began by telling her that I knew the nurses, as well as the social work department, might be contemplating not allowing Mary to take Eric home and possibly sending him to a foster home. She looked surprised. She asked me how I knew that information. I told her I overheard the nurses talking about it *(what I didn't tell her is that anyone could have guessed it.)* I went on to tell her that I was emancipated, and would take full responsibility for my nephew. I asked her take the necessary steps, so that Eric could come home with *me*. I was very surprised that Mary didn't open her mouth once to say anything except for when the social worker asked her if she agreed to this arrangement- she said yes.

Okay, now I can breathe, I said to myself. All of a sudden I became extremely anxious and apprehensive. Was I going to be able to keep this baby safe? How could I guarantee this? Am I doing the right thing for him, or am I doing this for me?

I think I had a bit of an anxiety attack. At that point, I looked at his little face and in to his beautiful big brown eyes and thought to myself; Susan, just do your best, and take it one day at a time.

The day finally came to take Eric and Mary home. I was both happy and nervous. I signed all the necessary paperwork. I was legally responsible for this baby's well-being and care. I felt tremendous responsibility. This was a new feeling for me. I didn't like it. It took the fun out of what was supposed to be a joyous occasion. It didn't matter before when I failed or made mistakes, but now, there is a little life depending on me for *everything,* and what is worse is that I have to keep him safe from his own mother. I felt as if I bit off much more then I could chew. I hope I did the right thing!

The Connor's were very gracious to take on this responsibly. I made sure that I thanked them, and told them how much I appreciated what they were doing for us, because without their help I might not have been able to take Eric home.

I began to get very over protective. Whenever any one of the Connor kids picked up the baby, I would be right there telling them they weren't holding him the right way or that they weren't feeding him properly. I didn't want anyone to hold, feed, or change him but me. I did like when Mary held him, which wasn't very often. I had to push him on her, and tell her how cute they looked together. There was one thing that I didn't like at all and that is she was a little too rough with him, and she'd get angry with him if he squirmed while she was changing his diaper, or if he fussed while she was trying to feed him. I tried to keep my mouth shut, but it was impossible. When I noticed that she was losing her patience with him, I would ask if I could finish the feeding, or diaper change. She would say "yeah" in a devilish tone of voice and practically throw him at me. The newness was wearing off and I was becoming afraid for my nephew's safety. The last time this happened, she stormed out the door and didn't show up again for four days. They were a relaxing four days though!

Eric slept in the bassinet that my mother bought for him, and I would sleep on the floor next to it so that I would wake up if he cried. One night, I woke up and Mary had the baby and was getting ready to leave the house. I asked her what she was doing and she said she was taking Eric for a walk.

"Mary," I said, "It's 3:00 in the morning, and it's freezing out. You can't take that baby out now!"

"He's *my* baby," she said. "I can do what ever the fuck I want with him. If you want a baby have one of your own!" I told her that I did what I did for *her,* not for me. I reminded her that I was the only reason that Eric was allowed to go home with her, and I went through a lot of trouble and expense to be emancipated, and taking two busses to work to prove to the courts that *I* was responsible enough to properly care for an infant wasn't easy. I also told her that it would have been a hell of a lot easier to have my own child. She placed Eric back in his bassinet. She turned to me and said, "Some night, you're not going to wake up, and I *am* going to take him. Then she stormed out the door. I didn't consider that a threat. I considered that a promise.

Eric was almost three weeks old. I took him to his first doctor's appointment. He had gained eight ounces since birth. I figured that I must have been doing something right. He's gaining weight, he doesn't have a rash or cradle cap and he was a fairly happy baby. He only fussed when his diaper needed changing or if he was hungry. I loved him so much, but boy was I tired!

Mary was gone for almost a week. She never even called to see how Eric was. Then one day the phone rang. It was Mary.

She asked to speak to me. When I got on the phone she began to scream profanities at me. She was calling me baby stealer, and bitch, and threatening to take Eric in the night. I told her that I was responsible for him, and if she ever did that I would call the police. She proceeded to tell me that the police would never find him. I took that as a direct threat to Eric's life. I knew then that I needed to sleep with one eye open at all times. Days rolled in to nights and back in to days again. I was so very tired from not sleeping soundly. I woke up to the littlest of noises. Until one night I just finally passed out.

I heard noises, but I thought I was dreaming. It was Mary. She had snuck in the house and she took Eric out of the bassinet. I caught her going out the front door with him. All he was wearing was a diaper, t-shirt and a receiving blanket. I jumped up and shouted to her; "What are you doing? Give me that baby! He is going to freeze to death!"

"Go have your own fuckin' baby," she said. "This is MY baby." I ran over and tried to grab him away from her. She held on to him. We began to struggle and Eric began to scream.

"You're hurting him," I yelled. "Give him to me!" She held on to him, and she had that evil smirk on her face. I realized at that moment that she didn't care about him. The only reason she continued to try and take him was to get back at me. Finally, Mrs. Connor came running out.

"Mary," she yelled! What are you doing! You let that baby go! If you want to leave and freeze to death then go right ahead. Susan is responsible for that baby and you are not taking him anywhere, now let him go or I will fuckin' kick the shit out of you!"

Mary *threw* him at me. I caught him in mid air. I wanted so badly to hit her at that moment. I couldn't let my mind wander to think about what would have happened if she had succeeded in sneaking him out of the house. I knew this wouldn't be the last time she would attempt to take him. He was no longer safe.

I knew what I had to do. I knew it would kill me, but this wasn't about *me*. This was about what was best and safest for my nephew. I picked up the phone and called the social worker and told her everything that has been going on, and that she needed to come and get my nephew because he was no longer safe. My heart was breaking. I felt like a biggest failure in the world.

I held Eric and cried until the social worker arrived with his new foster parent. I kissed him goodbye and told him I was so sorry I failed him and that I loved him with all of my heart. I handed him to Mrs. Connor because I couldn't bear to hand him over to a stranger- then I ran to the bedroom to cry.

I watched them out of the up-stairs bedroom window as they loaded Eric into the car and drove away. I felt as if my heart was going to stop beating. My life suddenly felt entirely empty-I missed him so much. I wanted to die just to get away from the anguish that I felt. I knew I did what was best for Eric, but that didn't ease the pain any. I was heart broken.

CHAPTER THIRTY-THREE

FINALLY EIGHTEEN

It was my eighteenth birthday, and as usual, nobody remembered except for the Connor's. I sat by the phone all day waiting for a call from my mother or Karen. It never came. Mrs. Connor felt so bad for me that she said, "Okay…we have a celebration tonight…we're all going to the Covered Wagon!"

This was a very big deal because Mrs. Connor NEVER got off the couch, not even to go to the bathroom! And if she did get up and go out somewhere (which was very rare) she wanted to be wheeled in a wheel chair. There wasn't anything wrong with her except for a severe case of laziness.

The covered wagon was a little hole in the wall nightclub that featured country bands. I wasn't much in the mood for partying. I missed Eric and my father. I was totally pissed at my mother, and of course, hurt. Life basically sucked. I just wanted to crawl under a rock and never come out!

I didn't like country music all that much at that particular time in my life, but the Connor's gesture was very thoughtful. Now, if they told me they were taking me to see an Aerosmith or Led Zeppelin tribute band I may have been a little bit more motivated.

A NICKEL IN MY SHOE

The drinking age was eighteen. I could actually legally drink. I didn't have to use Nana's ID anymore. That was, at the very least, good for a laugh.

It turned out to be a very fun night. I drank beer- which I hated, and danced to unfamiliar music all night long. And for my birthday song the band sang a tune called, *"Get Your Finger Out of It, It Don't Belong to You."* It was a blast actually. I went thinking I wasn't going to have a good time, and found it was one of the most memorable times of my life. It wasn't a matter of the place we were at, or the music we danced to. It was a matter of being with people who genuinely cared about me- being with the people that were always there for me when I needed them the most. They made my day special. They were my *real* family.

I woke up to the radio alarm the next morning and as I was lying in bed the song "New York, New York" came on the radio. I was lying there just listening, when I thought to myself; I want to go away. I want to start a new life. I think I'll go to California, but first I'll make a pit stop in Las Vegas. Everyone talks about how much fun it is there, and I'm sick and tired of being trapped. I want to live my own life.

I had saved up three thousand dollars, which I thought was plenty of money, got dressed and headed to the airport. I bought a one-way ticket to Las Vegas, Nevada. I was finally in control of my own life- no more abuse…so I thought.

EPILOGUE

There were many happy and joyous times in my life, as well as sad and heartbreaking times. Some of the time life was an adventure, at other times- a tragedy. The important thing was that I was, by age, allowed to be my own person, to make my own decisions, and to live my own life.

When I was only eighteen, I spent many nights homeless, and was forced to sleep on park benches. A very kind and generous man, who managed a small grocery store in Long Beach, would turn his back while I stole a candy bar or two. He put his own morals aside and allowed me to steal because he knew I was penniless and starving.

Then a break came when I was barely nineteen years old. Mr. Hoting, and his assistant Kathy, both bank managers, gave me a chance and hired me as a bank teller. They took me under their wing, and because of their generosity and faith I was able to turn my life around- for Kathy and Mr. Hoting I am grateful.

I am also so very thankful, (and feel blessed) for my very good friend Sherry. I don't know if I would have succeeded out there in this big and scary world all alone-without her. She gave me guidance, friendship and love. Sherry, her husband and her four beautiful children became my family when I had none. Thank you, from the bottom of my heart, Sherry and Carlos, for taking me in, sharing your family with me and not letting me fail or fall. Michael, Melina, Mia, and Marcus...Aunty Sue loves you! *(And just know that there was lots of love cooked in to all of those mac & cheese dinners!)*

There are so many people that I would like to thank for helping me in some way or another to be able to make it through another day of my childhood. Nancy A...thank you for coming in to my life. I didn't know how to laugh or even smile until I met you. You bring sunshine into people's lives, you have a gift. I miss you.

Deneane, we've been friends since thirteen- thank you for all the times you and your mother gave me a place to sleep when I didn't have a home. Thanks for being my friend and accepting me for who I was and who I am- and never judging me, or my life.

Chris G, thank you for have giving me the strength to make it through some of the most miserable days of my childhood- you gave me something (someone) to look forward to- thanks for being there.

Maribeth, thank you for having faith in me. We shared a lot of laughter and tears together. I miss you so much and wish for you all the good things that life has to offer- there isn't a person who deserves it more than you.

My mother and I made amends. It wasn't easy and it didn't happen overnight. I carried a chip on my shoulder for many years, which, in turn held me back from moving forward with my life. Harboring anger and resentment for all of those years made me a miserable and negative person. I got to the point where I didn't like myself because of the angry feelings that I felt everyday- all because I was waiting for acknowledgement and an apology that never came. I finally realized that it was *I* that had to either forgive my mother or feel this way forever. As I said- It wasn't easy and it took many years, but I changed my way of thinking and let all of my negative feelings go- and prayed that my mother would find peace, just as I have- in order to move on. It wasn't until after I *truly* forgave her that we became close- that we became best friends. My mother chose to live in a state of denial about all of the atrocities done to me as a child until on her deathbed in January of 2004. I was holding her hand as she laid dying and gasping for breath. She squeezed my hand, looked up at me and, with her whole heart, said "Sue, I'm so very sorry." I squeezed her hand back, and said I'm so sorry too Ma- I love you so much." She said "I love you too, and I'll see you soon." My mother closed her eyes and took her last breath. I know I said it once but I feel I must say it again...I would give *anything* to have my mother back.

When I was twenty-two, I married what I thought was a wonderful man. A man similar to what I described in one of my previous chapters. We had four beautiful children together, but he changed as the marriage wore on. After many years of psychological abuse of me, as well as physical abuse of my children, I filed for divorce. I was married for almost 20 years.

I remarried in 2006, to a man opposite my first husband. He is patient, gentle and kind. I love him very much.

Even though we lived thousands of miles apart for many years (until I moved back to RI to help take care of my mother in 1994) Karen and I remained very close. We even went to nursing school together. We would fall asleep talking and giggling on the phone with each other *every* night. She was my very best friend. Karen passed away, three years ago- on February 26, 2008, from breast cancer at the age of forty-three. As a matter of fact, she passed three years ago tonight as I write this epilogue.

I was honored that she allowed me to hold her hand and lay beside her in her most private moment. The last words she heard were my whispers in her ear telling her that I love her more then life itself, I would see her again in Heaven someday, and that I was so sorry that I couldn't save her this time. This is what haunted me the very most about her terminal illness- I couldn't save her. I begged and pleaded with God to trade places with her. I would have given *anything* to take the pain for her. I felt helpless, and that is one of the most terrible feelings that anyone could ever experience.

My life will never be the same without my little sister. I miss her every second of every day. I'll never laugh with anyone like I did with her. No one will ever understand me and give me advice and guidance like she did. My life is so lonely and empty without her. Karen always was, and always will be, my Angel.

My sister Mary gave in to the voices once again and jumped from a sixteen-story building. This time it ended her life. She was only 24-years-old. *(I was visiting my mother and Karen one beautiful summer night in July of 1983, when Mary arrived at the door. She asked if Karen and I would style her hair and apply her make-up. Of course Karen and I said yes. Both Karen and I were so happy because Mary was happy-which was extremely rare. (Little did we know that a sudden elevation in mood is one of the major tell tale signs of someone about to commit suicide.) We had so much fun together! All three of us were laughing and joking with one another. Mary had the most gorgeous hair, we curled it- I've never seen it look so beautiful! Then we applied her make-up. I never before saw her look so pretty- or act so happy. She then kissed both of us (which was odd) and left the house- we assumed to take the bus home. The next morning, at about 7:00am, the phone began to ring. It was various people calling to give us their condolences for the death of my sister. We were sure that they were prank calls because Mary was so elated the night before- when she*

EPILOGUE

*left my mothers house to take the bus home. "How could she be dead?"
We were thinking. And if she really was dead, the police would have
notified us. What Mary actually did after leaving the house was not at
all what we thought. Mary took the bus to an assisted living facility in
Providence- rode the elevator to the sixteenth floor, walked down to the
end of the hallway, removed the screen from the window, and without
hesitation- jumped to her death. She landed on the cement directly in
front of two elderly ladies that were sitting on a bench beneath the window she jumped from. There were five suicides in the city that Friday
night and due to all the confusion, we were never notified. One officer
thought his partner notified us and vice versa- hence the condolence
phone calls the next morning. Karen and I had to go to the city morgue
to identify Mary that afternoon. Identifying our sister on a slab in the
morgue was the most horrifying, sad and difficult task that either of us
ever had to do in our entire lives. Karen and I gave Mary one last gift;
we, once again, styled her hair and applied her make-up for both her
wake and funeral services.)*

I immediately (and repeatedly) called the state in an
attempt to get Eric back but he was placed up for adoption the
minute my sister died.

I searched for my nephew Eric for thirty years. Then, in
2009, a 'birth Angel' found him for me. He looks *exactly* like
my sister Mary, but he has a complete opposite personality. He
is kind, gentle and warm. He's funny and very intelligent. He
currently resides in Alabama with his wife Missy and their children. (They even have a grandchild!) I haven't had the pleasure
of meeting him yet. Someday we will meet face to face, but for
now we will have to settle with talking on the phone. I'm so
very happy to have him back in my life.

There is one person that I'd like to mention here. I didn't
talk about him in my book too much, because I didn't know

him very well at that time in my life. His name was Anthony. He was my mother's common law husband, and one of the greatest men that I have ever known. He came in to a very troubled family and hung in there for 30 years. He was the *only* one to try to convince me to return to school-to go somewhere, and to be somebody. We put him through hell sometimes, but he never gave up on us. He was one in a million. He was so dedicated to my mother. He took such excellent care of her when she was dying and *never* complained. When my ex-husband left me with four young children, emptied the bank accounts, and I was trying to make it through nursing school- Anthony was the only one to offer to take me and my four children in. When I told him I didn't know what I was going to do, or where we were going to live, Anthony said "you are going to come here to live- of course!" He was kind enough to allow us to live with him even after my mother died in 2004.

Anthony passed away in 2007 from a brain tumor. He died just eight months before Karen. Anthony was my savior; he was my rock. I miss him so much.

As for me... I currently reside in Florida with my husband and four children. I work as a psychiatric nurse as well as volunteer for the Rape Crisis and Abuse Shelter.

I must admit that life is still very frightening for me at times. I had a heart attack one month to the day of Anthony dying- I was only forty-five years old. What worries me the most is- if I fall, my children fall as well. I'm the only one of my immediate family remaining. At times it feels as if the weight of the world is on my shoulders and that nobody cares or understands. Every now and then I'll wake up in cold sweat thinking about what would happen to my children if I could no longer provide, or care for them. A week before Karen died she said to me, "Oh Susan, I don't know what sucks worse, to be *you,* or to be *me.*" I just lay in her lap and cried.

Life, without a doubt, can be very difficult at times. I have to work very hard, everyday, at keeping a positive attitude. Some days are definitely better than others. What I have found is that helping people less fortunate than myself helps me to see that things aren't really as bad as they seem- there are people worse off than I am. Helping others is healing. Everyone is special- everyone has a gift to share. What seems like a small and insignificant gesture to you, may be monumental to the person you are helping. It doesn't have to cost money- donate your time, knowledge or your talent. It can be something as simple as a smile, a kind word or a compliment that makes a person's day brighter. When I am teaching the nursing assistants, I *always* remind them that some of the elderly people that they are caring for have no family or friends left in this world, and theirs is the *only* smile that they *ever* see or kind word that they *ever* hear. Try it. Do something nice for someone- see how wonderful it makes you feel about yourself. A smile and a kind gesture or word not is not only healing but is absolutely contagious as well!

I want to let everyone reading this book to know that you *can* overcome most, if not *all* hardships in your life. I was left homeless, with no food or money- in nursing school with four small kids to house, clothe and feed. I succeeded with the help of some very kind and generous people; my nursing instructor, Mrs. Norquist, gave me the time off that I needed to get my life together so that I could continue on in the nursing program and not have to resign. Peggy, my babysitter-told me she wouldn't leave me stranded, even though I had no money to pay her. Maribeth, my savior, thank you for having faith in me and giving me the opportunity of a lifetime in your surgical practice- You are one of the most sweet and non-judgmental people that I have ever met in my entire life. You look for the good in everyone. I'm so thankful that you're my friend. I love you. Mas and Selina, were the *only* friends who offered to help me move out of my house- the *only* friends that didn't run and hide. You truly learn who your real friends are in trying times. Keep the true friends- let the fair weather friends go! There is a saying that I try to live by: "If you're going to be a friend, be a good one."

Never give up. When you fall, pick yourself up, dust yourself off and continue on. Keep smiling! Do not let anyone ever get the best of you. My ex-mother in law, as well as my ex-husband, told me that I would never make it through college because I was too stupid.

I thought to myself, "I'll show them! I put my fears aside and went on to graduate at the top of my class. I had both of them to thank for my success. Instead of allowing them to break me, I used their negativity to motivate me. Yes, I worked extremely hard in college, but they were my *motivating factor* in the first two programs I graduated from- Surgical Technology and Emergency Medical Technology. Remember, my last formal year in school was sixth-grade. If I can do it so can you! Every time I wanted to quit, I would see their faces, and hear their voices telling me how stupid I am and how I will never make it- or I'd see my (ex) husband in a fit of laughter because he thought the idea of me going to school was a hilarious joke.

When I went through nursing school, *my kids* were my motivating factor. Children- and the thought of not being able to feed them, can be a very strong motivator. My mother died

212

during my and Karen's last semester of nursing school. Karen told me she was utterly heartbroken and didn't think she would be able to finish the last semester. I said to her, "Karen, we have to go on. We have to make Ma proud. She's watching us. *I* have to go on because I have four children to feed- beside that, I don't want to live the rest of my life working three minimum wage jobs just to make ends meet. No thank you! We *are* finishing nursing school...no matter what it takes."

No matter how hard life seems, there are support groups and various other organizations that will help you to get on your feet, or that will help you change your situation. Easy? No. Possible? Absolutely! There is an old saying, "anything worth having is hard work." I will not sugar coat anything-some life situations are pretty tough but this is not the 1960's anymore. There are many programs and support groups to help you along the way- no matter what your needs are. Always remember that you are not alone. There are people who care and more than that, you can do *anything* you put your mind to! I was 42 years-old when I graduated from nursing school. You're *never* too old! And what's more is that education is something that no one can *ever* take away from you-you earn it, you own it-for life! Almost everyone needs a motivating factor, and it's different for everyone-find yours-once you do there will be no stopping you. Never give up-never stop dreaming...and... never stop smiling!

On one last note...for our most defenseless- most cherished members of our society; Infants, Children, Elderly, and Animals...

Be aware. Be vigilant. Be their voice when they are too afraid to speak. Be their advocate when they are powerless against their "caregivers" strength.

Open your eyes- don't be blind to their bruises- on the inside as well as the outside. It shouldn't hurt to be alive.

Look into their eyes...the windows to the soul... Are they begging you to notice? Are they pleading with you to care... to save them...to give them strength...To give them hope? To provide them with safety? Love and belonging? ...A fair chance to succeed at life?

Open your ears- do you hear their silent screams- Begging to be rescued...Don't turn your back- don't look the other way...

Be brave- be someone's hero. It only takes empathy, caring and one anonymous phone call.

Open your heart and you could save a precious life.

EPILOGUE

"Never look down on anyone, unless
you're helping them up"
Jesse Jackson